Essential Histories

The Napoleonic Wars

The rise of the Emperor 1805–1807

Todd Fisher

OSPREY
PUBLISHING

First published in Great Britain in 2001 by Osprey Publishing,
Elms Court, Chapel Way, Botley, Oxford OX2 9LP
E-mail: info@ospreypublishing.com

ISBN 1 84176 205 9

Editor: Rebecca Cullen
Designer: Ken Vail Graphic Design, Cambridge, UK
Picture research by Image Select International
Cartography by The Map Studio
Index by Alan Rutter
Origination by Grasmere Digital Imaging, Leeds, UK
Printed and bound in China by L. Rex Printing Company Ltd
01 02 03 04 05   10 9 8 7 6 5 4 3 2 1

For a complete list of titles available
from Osprey Publishing please contact:

Osprey Direct UK, P.O. Box 140,
Wellingborough, Northants NN8 4ZA, UK
Email: info@ospreydirect.co.uk

Osprey Direct USA, P.O. Box 130,
Sterling Heights, MI 48311-0130, USA
Email: info@ospreydirectusa.com

Or visit Osprey at:
www.ospreypublishing.com

Contents

Chronology

1802 **2 August** Napoleon proclaimed Consul for life

1803 **20 May** War breaks out between France and Britain

1804 **21 March** Execution of the Duc d'Enghien
19 May Creation of the Marshalate
2 December Napoleon's coronation as Emperor of the French

1805 **25 August** *Grande Armée* leaves Boulogne for Germany
9 October Ney forces the Danube at Gunzburg
14 October Ney closes the door on the Austrian army at Elchingen
19 October Mack and the Austrian army capitulate at Ulm
21 October Battle of Trafalgar
30 October Massena fights Archduke Charles at Caldiero
10 November Mortier escapes destruction at Durenstein
2 December Battle of Austerlitz
26 December Austria makes peace in the Treaty of Pressburg

1806 **23 January** Pitt dies after hearing the news of Austerlitz
14 February Massena leads the invasion of Naples
30 March Napoleon's brother Joseph is proclaimed King of Naples
5 June Napoleon's brother Louis is proclaimed King of Holland
4 July Battle of Maida: minor British victory in the south of Italy
12 July Creation of the Confederation of the Rhine
6 August Holy Roman Empire is dissolved
9 August Prussia begins to mobilize for war
7 October Napoleon receives the Prussian ultimatum; he crosses the border the next day
10 October Battle of Saalfield; Lannes defeats Archduke Ferdinand
14 October Twin battles of Jena and Auerstädt
27 October Napoleon enters Berlin
21 November In the 'Berlin Decrees' Napoleon institutes the Continental Blockade
28 November French troops enter Warsaw
26 December Battles of Pultusk and Golymin

1807 **8 February** Battle of Eylau
21 March A British adventure in Egypt ends in defeat at Damietta
27 May Selim III dethroned in Turkey
10 June Battle of Heilsberg
14 June Battle of Friedland
7 July Defeat at Buenos Aires ends a British invasion of the Argentine
7 July Treaties of Tilsit between France, Russia and Prussia
7 September Copenhagen surrenders to a British army

Napoleon in the Battle of Jena (by Vernet).
(AKG London)

A temporary peace

When Napoleon Bonaparte signed the Peace of Amiens on 25 March 1802, he became the most popular man in France. Not only had the crown of victory constantly sat upon his brow as he had defeated one enemy army after another – the Piedmontese, the Austrians, the Mamelukes, the Turks and the Austrians again – but now he gave France what she really wanted: peace.

Peace allowed First Consul Bonaparte to put France's domestic house in order. He reorganized the laws of the land, the economy and the education system. Earlier in the year he had established freedom of religion, and his treaty, or Concordat, with the Pope had finally brought religious peace.

The Treaty of Amiens, 1802

The Treaty of Amiens between France and Britain ended the last of the wars of the French Revolution. It represented a defeat for William Pitt the Younger, but he was more than happy to see the blame for it fall on his successor as Tory Prime Minister, Henry Addington. Pitt never regarded the peace as anything other than a pause in a continuing power struggle with France. But Great Britain needed time. She had lost or alienated many of her potential and traditional allies. Austria had been badly mauled by France in the last war as a result of the battles of Marengo and Hohenlinden. Russia appeared on the verge of an alliance with France. Denmark had been thrown into France's arms by the unprovoked British attack on the Danish fleet at Copenhagen in 1801. Prussia coveted Hanover, a British crown possession and home of the royal house, and had also been offended by Britain's behavior in the Baltic. Britain was somewhat isolated as a result. More vexing to Pitt and his friends was their perception that France had violated the spirit of the Peace of Amiens by absorbing

Signing of the Louisiana Purchase. This vast sale of land to the United States put much-needed money in the hands of France in return for a territory that Napoleon saw as indefensible. (Hulton Getty)

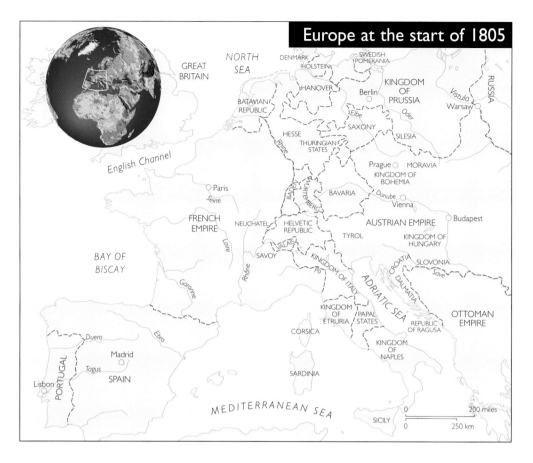

parts of Italy and interfering in the internal affairs of Switzerland.

Following the treaty, France quickly made peace with the Turks. Britain viewed this with alarm as a possible threat to India or Egypt. She countered by refusing to withdraw from Malta, a specific violation of the peace accord. Addington even went so far as to say that every gain made by France should be countered by a concession given to Britain. Bonaparte stirred up discontent among the British merchants by charging a higher tariff on British goods than French. French trade rose by 50 percent in the year following the treaty and the British middle class saw little advantage in continuing a military peace that was coupled to a trade war.

No more a believer that peace would last than Pitt, Bonaparte took advantage of the respite to expand the French fleet, further threatening recent British naval dominance. The sale of Louisiana to the Americans in

1803 brought 80 million francs into the French treasury. Bonaparte also made largely unsuccessful and somewhat shameful efforts to reestablish the French colonies in the Caribbean. While these attempts would ultimately prove a failure, they caused great alarm in the British Parliament.

Seeing no advantage in maintaining the peace, the British ambassador to France, Sir Charles Whitworth, gave an ultimatum to Bonaparte to evacuate Holland and Switzerland. This was refused as being outside of the treaty's terms. France then countered by offering to have the Tsar, Alexander of Russia, who had plans for the islands himself, mediate the question of Malta; this was refused in turn, further alienating the Russians. But the tide would soon turn in Britain's favor. Following the withdrawal of the British ambassador in May 1803, Addington broke the Peace of Amiens by seizing French ships without giving a

Napoleon Bonaparte as First Consul. First Consul was his office after he seized power in the Brumaire coup. In 1800 he won the Battle of Marengo, which led to the establishment of his Imperial reign. (Hulton Getty)

This led the Bourbon reactionaries to take extreme measures. The Bourbons felt that since they were God's appointed, any measures to reestablish themselves on the throne of France were justified, including assassination. No fewer than 11 plots or attempts on Bonaparte's life were made and failed, and considerable controversy remains as to whether he ultimately died of natural causes.

Bonaparte recognized that if he intended to live long enough to achieve his goals, he would have to put a stop to the Bourbons' assassination bureau. He established a police department to spy on his enemies under the supervision of the notorious Joseph Fouché, who was a former priest, a terrorist and a man well known for his corrupt nature, but

declaration of war. This infuriated Bonaparte, who ordered the arrest of all British citizens currently in France. While he had been provoked, the monarchs of Europe, biased against Republican France anyway, viewed Bonaparte's act as criminal.

Napoleon the Emperor

Bonaparte's popularity in France had one potential drawback. As the prospects of a popular revolt against him faded, the former ruling family of France, the Bourbons, became more desperate. At several points during the period of the Directory (1795–99), France had seemed on the verge of restoring the monarchy. But now all hope was fading, for the First Consul's government shone in comparison to the Directory that it replaced.

William Pitt the Younger. Although early in his career he espoused liberal ideas, as head of the government 1784–1801 and 1804–06 he increasingly employed repressive measures. As an implacable enemy of Napoleon and the Revolution, it was said that the news of Austerlitz led to his death. (Ann Ronan Picture Library)

who was highly qualified for the job. He pressured neutral states into evicting the troublesome émigrés who had been operating with near impunity along France's borders. Finally, he learned that the young Duc d'Enghien was in Baden planning to lead an insurrection against him. Bonaparte's Foreign Minister, Charles Maurice Talleyrand, convinced him to send out a raiding party to capture Enghien as a way to strike against the Bourbons. As a result, on 10 March 1804, a group of dragoons rode into Ettenheim, abducted the young duke and quickly brought him back to the château of Vincennes outside Paris. A quick

The Duc d'Enghien, kidnapped on Napoleon's orders at Baden, which was neutral territory, and executed in the moat of the château of Vincennes. (Ann Ronan Picture Library)

court-martial found Enghien guilty of being in English pay and planning an invasion, and he was executed in the early morning of 21 March 1804.

This act was a turning point of Bonaparte's career. The execution of a prince galvanized the monarchies of Europe against him. It can be argued that Bonaparte had little choice but to send the message to the Bourbons that two could play at the game of murder. In fact, the assassination plots against Bonaparte dwindled considerably after this event.

At this juncture the First Consul for Life decided that his best security lay in having a hereditary title. At the urging of many of his closest advisers, Bonaparte introduced a bill into the Senate declaring the French Empire. This was passed in May 1804 and overwhelmingly approved by a plebiscite

put to the French people. So it was that First Consul Bonaparte became Napoleon I, Emperor of the French. His coronation ceremony took place at Notre Dame on 2 December 1804, with the Pope presiding. The symbolic height of the ceremony occurred when Napoleon placed the crown upon his own head, further antagonizing the European dynasties, who regarded him as 'the usurper'.

A death in St Petersburg

The Russian nobility had been shifting towards the British camp for some time. The previous Tsar, Paul, had been on the verge of allying Russia with Napoleon's Republic, alarming both the Russian aristocracy and the British, so the British envoy extraordinary to Russia, Sir Charles Whitworth, helped hatch a plot for the removal of the francophile Tsar. A number of disgruntled nobles and generals fell in with the plot and assassinated Tsar Paul on 11 March 1801. The new Tsar, Paul's son Alexander, was aware of the plot and became beholden to the conspirators. From the complex feelings of guilt regarding his father's murder, Alexander would develop something of a messianic complex

wherein he played the role of savior of Christian Europe.

Over the next few years, relations between Russia and France deteriorated. Alexander saw every move on the part of the French as a threat to the areas of the Mediterranean over which he claimed a protectorate. Despite some false moves by the British, Alexander gradually drew closer to a British alliance. The execution of the Duc d'Enghien was the telling event. After this, Alexander joined with Britain in forming the Third Coalition in April 1805, and was rewarded with a lavish British subsidy.

Efforts were now made to get Austria to join the coalition. While Austria had met Napoleon twice before in war and been humiliated, Napoleon's consolidation of northern Italy was a direct threat to Austrian interests. Austria had been building up her armies for several years. When Napoleon crowned himself the King of Northern Italy in March 1805, this was too much. Austria joined the Third Coalition in August of that year, and received a generous subsidy too. The stage was now set for one of history's greatest campaigns.

Tsar Alexander. After the murder of his father, Alexander took over the vast Russian Empire. While he was a most eccentric ruler, he expanded its holdings until after the end of the Napoleonic Wars, when he went mad and abdicated to follow the life of a monk. (Ann Ronan Picture Library)

Napoleon's coronation, 2 December 1804. In a ceremony presided over by the Pope, Napoleon placed the crown on both Josephine's and his own head. (AKG London)

The armies prepare

With Britain renewing the war in the late spring of 1803, Napoleon went about reorganizing his army for the possible invasion of England. He sent orders to his Chief of Staff, Alexander Berthier, to prepare camps for his Army Corps at Bolougne. Here they would train and prepare for the time that the English Channel was clear of British ships and invasion could take place.

France

Napoleon organized his army incorporating the ideas of French military theorists of the previous generation. He was the first to attempt to use a permanent corps structure. Prior to the French Revolution, any organization above the brigade was temporary. The French had established permanent divisions to great effect during the wars of the French Revolution (1792–1801). Now Napoleon decided to create permanent corps that were in effect miniature armies, each with its own cavalry and artillery complements attached to two or three infantry divisions. The success of this structure can be shown by the fact that modern armies use the same organization in a largely unaltered form.

The French corps had a permanent staff attached. Commanders would learn to know their subordinates. Divisions would become accustomed to maneuvering in conjunction with their sister divisions. The Light Cavalry, attached to the corps, went through exercises that brought a higher degree of cooperation than any other army in the world enjoyed.

European armies consisted of a series of building blocks. Infantry regiments were made up of battalions, which in turn were comprised of companies. A brigade consisted of regiments, and divisions were composed

Alexander Berthier. As Napoleon's Chief of Staff, he stayed by the Emperor's side until his first abdication in 1814. He was said to be the only man in the Empire who could keep up with and understand Napoleon's mind. (Photo Musee de l'armée, Paris)

of two or more brigades. On top of this, Napoleon added infantry corps of two or more infantry divisions with one or two cavalry brigades attached.

Napoleon had infantry of two types, line (*ligne*) and light (*légère*). The light infantry, more than the line, tended to be used for skirmishing, reconnaissance and rearguard protection. Infantry battalions at this time were made up of nine companies: seven center companies and two elite companies;

the latter were a *voltigeur* (light) company and a grenadier or carabinier company, depending on whether it was a line or light battalion. In 1805, Napoleon stripped the elite companies from a number of regiments left in garrison to form an elite division under General Oudinot. This formation became known as Oudinot's grenadiers.

The light cavalry attached to the infantry corps was one of two types, either hussars or chasseurs. These were functionally the same outside of their dress, although the hussars generally had the better reputation, due in part to their dashing appearance.

Napoleon then created the Cavalry Reserve Corps from the line cavalry (dragoons) and the heavy cavalry regiments (cuirassiers and carabiniers). Their intent was to act as the 'arm of rupture', to be committed to break an enemy that had been worn down by the infantry. To a lesser extent they could be used to stabilize a situation that was getting out of hand. To accompany these heavy cavalry were batteries of horse artillery, whose 8pdr guns could be brought quickly into position and deliver tremendous hitting power. The combination of these two arms was extremely hard to resist.

Napoleon, having trained as an artillerist himself, aided by fine gunners like Marmont, had implemented many improvements that greatly increased the power of the French artillery. Better, lighter and more mobile guns, better gunpowder, better training and better tactics gave France a major superiority in this field.

One problem for the French in the 1805 campaign was that they did not have enough mounts for their dragoons. Therefore, one division of dragoons had to fight dismounted as infantry. They would not prove to be effective as infantry, but they eventually received their horses from captured stocks.

Finally there was the Imperial Guard Corps. These elite men combined the two Guard infantry regiments (the grenadiers and chasseurs of foot), the Guard cavalry (the grenadiers, carabiniers and chasseurs of horse) and the flying horse artillery batteries. The Guard acted as a final reserve and as the force that would deliver the *coup de grâce*.

In 1803, as this army formed in its various camps, Napoleon was making preparations for an invasion of England. He had barges built and began to stockpile large quantities of supplies for the anticipated campaign. While the invasion would never occur, the intensive training that the men received over a two-year period would hone this army into a superb fighting machine.

When France was declared an Empire, Napoleon quickly adapted many of his creations into Imperial ones. As First Consul he had created the Legion of Honor. This now became a method of rewarding people who had excelled in their field – a sort of minor nobility, but one based on merit. Along the same lines, Napoleon now created the Marshalate. Originally, 18 generals became marshals. They were chosen for their ability and either for their personal loyalty or because they represented a political or military faction that Napoleon wished to win over. The military factions were made up of members of the army who had served in an army not commanded by Napoleon. These were many of the men who would lead Napoleon's Corps in the following years. With these titles came a large salary. To become a marshal was the aspiration of every French soldier. The phrase 'There is a marshal's baton in every knapsack' was more than just propaganda, for some of Napoleon's marshals had indeed come up through the ranks.

The life of a French soldier was very hard by modern standards. The soldiers on campaign slept on the ground, wrapped in their bedroll. The French had learned that to carry tents and other camp baggage slowed the army down considerably. Unless the army went into winter quarters, it was generally frowned upon to billet inside a house, although this rule was violated frequently and did not apply to higher-grade officers.

The soldier received 24 ounces (680g) of bread each day and 8 ounces (227g) of meat. In addition, there were vegetables and wine. The meat and legumes were pooled and most often turned into a soup or stew. These were the official rations, and the soldiers were free to buy other items from the locals, *vivandières* or *cantinières*. There was also pillage or loot from the surrounding countryside, although this was discouraged in varying degrees by the different marshals, Davout being the strictest, and Massena perhaps the most slack.

If required, the infantry could march 20 miles (32km) a day or more. The soldiers of this French army could achieve this rate with astoundingly low rates of attrition. It was in no small part a result of their training, for later less-trained armies of Napoleon would not come close to this standard.

While Napoleon had his headquarters and two of his corps near Boulogne – the 4th Corps under Marshal Soult, the largest in the army, and the 5th Corps under Marshal Lannes – the remainder of the army was spread along the coastline. Marshal Bernadotte's 1st Corps was in Hanover. General and future Marshal Marmont's 2nd Corps was in Utrecht. Marshal Davout's 3rd Corps was in Bruges. Marshal Ney's 6th Corps was in Montreuil. Marshal Augereau's 7th Corps was at Bayonne. Finally, there were cavalry camps in which Marshal Murat oversaw the formation of his cavalry reserve. These were located in Amiens, Bayonne, Bruges, Compiègne, Montreuil, and Nijmegen.

Let us view Napoleon's corps commanders. Marshal Bernadotte, in command of the 1st Corps, was a veteran of the Revolutionary Wars, where he had distinguished himself as much for his political intrigues as for his fighting ability. He was personally brave, while often hesitant to commit his command to battle. He had been in opposition to Napoleon's seizure of power in 1799, and had plotted against him with General Moreau in the Affair of the Placards in 1802. Bernadotte's erratic behavior under the Empire, in which he was entrusted with commands after repeated failures, was initially protected by a strong following among the Republicans, but

was ultimately saved by his marriage to Desirée Clary, Napoleon's former fiancée and sister to Joseph Bonaparte's wife, Julie. As a brother-in-law by marriage, Bernadotte would be spared the wrath that he would so often deserve – and he would ultimately reward Napoleon with betrayal.

General Marmont of the 2nd Corps was one of Napoleon's few friends. He had shown great organizational skills. He showed a particular talent for the artillery. It would be under him that the artillery reforms of 'Year 11' or 1804 would take place. It shows Napoleon's high opinion of him that he was the only non-marshal to command a corps in the *Grande Armée*.

Marshal Davout was to earn himself renown in the years 1805–07. He was the youngest of the original marshals. Totally devoted to Napoleon and France, he was a shrewd tactician and a harsh disciplinarian and did not suffer fools gladly. The result was that, although respected by his men and immediate subordinates, he was unpopular with his equals.

Marshal Soult was considered the best organizer in the army. He would make his 4th Corps the envy of the world. It was significantly larger than any other corps and was made up of some of the best fighting units in Europe. Soult had been a hero during the Revolution. He had fought determinedly in actions on the Rhine, in Flanders and in Italy. He always led from the front. In 1800 he was attempting a breakout from encircled Genoa when he received a near fatal wound. This would change him for ever. Never again would he be so cavalier in exposing himself to enemy fire. This meant that at times he was too far from the action to react quickly to opportunities at the front. In 1805, however, this was not yet known.

Marshal Lannes of the 5th Corps is considered in detail on pp. 82–85. Marshal Ney had a deserved reputation as a fiery leader. He had been in the thick of the fighting during the Revolutionary campaigns on the Rhine and in Flanders. He had never served under Bonaparte, and worse had been a friend of the 'traitor' Moreau, but his fortune was assured when he married one of the Empress Josephine's favorite ladies-in-waiting. He had the confidence to project victory in everything he did, and that attitude played well with the Emperor. When the marshals' batons were being handed out, Ney was considered the most trustworthy among the former Army of the Rhine generals. For these reasons, he received command of the 6th Corps and became a marshal.

Marshal Augereau had served with Bonaparte in Italy and had played a critical role in holding off one wing of the Austrian army, while Napoleon had crushed the other at the Battle of Castiglione. This, coupled with his avowed Republican sentiments, was sufficient to earn Augereau his marshalate and the 7th Corps command. Augereau was a braggart and somewhat of a bully. He had floated from one soldier-of-fortune job to the next until the French Revolution had given him the opportunity to rise. He was a rapacious looter and scoundrel, but he knew how to fight when cornered.

Marshal Murat was now Napoleon's brother-in-law after marrying his sister Caroline. He was the *Beau Idéal* of the cavalry; dashing, daring, leading from the front, and dressed in the most flamboyant uniforms of the army. He had limited intelligence, but had a killer eye for the timing of a cavalry charge. Vain and frivolous, he always seized the day and had been instrumental in Bonaparte's successes in the Vendémiaire uprising and the coup of Brumaire. He had been with Bonaparte throughout all of his campaigns and had served him well.

Several other commanders deserve our attention. The most important of them is Marshal Massena. He had been an army commander before Bonaparte and resented being forced to take a subservient role to him in 1796. He soon came to appreciate the 'Little Corporal's' talents. He fought by his side in 1796–97 and remained in Europe while the expedition to Egypt took place. He won great fame at the Battle of Zurich in 1799, when he destroyed a Russian–Austrian army under Rimsky-Korsakov. This caused

the Russians to withdraw from the Second Coalition and set the table for Bonaparte's return, the *coup d'état* of Brumaire, and victorious Marengo campaign. While Napoleon was descending on the rear of the Austrian army under Melas in 1800, Massena was doggedly holding Genoa. Here he made superhuman efforts to hold out until Bonaparte could make the winning maneuver. In 1805, Massena may have been the best man in France to command an army apart from the Emperor. He would square off in northern Italy against Austria's best commander, Archduke Charles. While highly skilled as an army leader, Massena had a deserved reputation for being the worst looter in the French army, for his libertine lifestyle required constant sustenance. It seems his attitudes never changed after his early life as a smuggler.

Marshals Mortier and Lefevbre were both daunting fellows; no thinkers but possessed with a determination to forge ahead into the thickest of the fighting. They were admired by their men and competent only under the direct eye of the Emperor. Both men would command corps during the campaigns of 1805–07.

Marshal Bessières had been by Napoleon's side for much of his time as a commander. He was a noble of the *ancien régime* and brought an air of class to the Imperial entourage. A stickler for detail and dress, Bessières would lead the Guard for many of the campaigns, where his renown for courage was coupled with a reputation for being priggish.

Marshal Brune had been one of the most devoted Republicans. He was given his marshalate to help mollify that faction. He commanded the army that defeated a Russo-British army under the Duke of York in 1799 in Holland. He had a Reserve Corps created around him to protect the coast against a British invasion once the *Grande Armée* moved inland.

As 1805 wore on and France's navy had not the slightest prospect of clearing the English Channel, Napoleon recognized that he would have to deal with the continental threats of Russia and Austria before he could once more turn his attention to the British. When Austria declared war, Napoleon made his move. The 'Army of the Ocean Coast' became the *Grande Armée*. He issued orders and on 31 August the well-oiled military machine turned its back on the Channel and marched towards the Austrian and Russian threat.

Austria

The Austrian army that awaited Napoleon was in a state of confusion, still reeling from the debacles of the First and the Second Coalitions. In these wars, the armies of the French Revolution and Consulate continually outperformed their Habsburg counterparts. The problems that confronted the armies of the Holy Roman Emperor, Francis II, were broad: logistically, tactically, strategically, and politically, the armies suffered handicaps compared to the rapidly modernizing French. The army of the Empress Maria Theresa of Austria had held off the greatest general of his day, Frederick the Great of Prussia. Her artillery was the envy of the world, and the infantry and cavalry accounted well for themselves. Following the Seven Years War (1756–63), a number of 'reforms' were attempted. The worst of these was an overhaul of the artillery arm. The result was a disaster, with several humiliating defeats at the hands of the Turks. Attempts to redress this situation succeeded only partially. Austria had the best artillery of the continental allies, but it could not compare to that of the French.

Throughout the reigns of the Emperors Joseph and Leopold, a number of changes were attempted in the infantry. Light infantry regiments were raised in 1798, but disbanded in 1801. The Habsburg commanders had no faith in the average troops performing well when not under the direct supervision of their officers. There were *Jäger* battalions (elite rifle-armed light troops) and the *Grenz* troops (hardy frontiersmen from the Balkans with a traditional duty of military service), but there were never enough to counter the French swarm of skirmishers. To compound the problem, the Austrians were introducing greater discipline into the *Grenzer* to ensure their political reliability and make them more compatible with the rest of their army, but suppressing their old flair for irregular warfare.

The problems faced by the Austrian Emperor were in large part due to past Habsburg successes. Primarily through marriages they had acquired many provinces with varied ethnic and racial populations. Therefore, no universal language existed in the army. Further, many of these provinces owed no loyalty to the Austrians, just to the Emperor personally. This meant that the Hungarians, for example, believed they could decide among themselves how much they would support the war effort. As the Empire was teetering on bankruptcy in 1805, the regiments were dispersed to minimize the costs of upkeep and to aid recruitment. Whatever its economic advantages, such dispersal meant that mobilization was a long process.

The Emperor's brother, the Archduke Charles, had set about reforming the army in 1801. He had taken power from the Hofkriegsrat, a military/civilian assembly, and had streamlined the logistical procedures. He was unquestionably Austria's best field commander, but he had a knack of alienating the court personalities and the ossified high command. He had close favorites whom he allowed to dictate to others considered above their station. Charles was constantly at odds with a series of foreign ministers and a combination of his enemies worked to remove him from his position of power. They launched a two-front attack, playing on Francis's paranoia regarding his brother's popularity, while urging him to join the alliance against Napoleon. Charles was adamant that the army was in no shape to fight the French and that Austria needed further peace to get her financial house in order. To that end he even advocated recognizing Napoleon's

General Mack. Despite defeat and capture while on loan to the Neapolitan army in 1805, Mack still appeared to the Austrians as the model of a modern scientific soldier and much was expected of him. (Roger-Viollet)

imperial status, humiliating as that might be for the oldest ruling family in Europe.

Charles, by advocating peace, gave his opposition an opening. Pitt, succeeding Addington as British Prime Minister in May 1804, offered subsidies and lavished bribes around the Viennese court, and Charles's enemies pounced. First they persuaded Francis to reinstate the Hofkriegsrat, then they stripped Charles's allies of their offices and commands. Finally, they advocated General Mack von Leiberich as a counterweight to Charles on military matters. Mack advocated joining the alliance and going to war. While Charles said the army was not ready, Mack's soothing words to Francis dismissed such worries. When Britain provided the required subsidies, the die was cast. Francis joined the alliance and Charles was assigned to the nominal 'main

theater' of Italy, while Mack took the largest army and in the late summer of 1805 prepared to invade Bavaria.

Mack chose this ill-suited time to reorganize the infantry regiments. He changed their existing structure, three battalions of six companies each, into four battalions of four companies. To complete the confusion, Mack did not provide for properly trained higher commanders for the extra battalions. That Mack attempted this change on the eve of war shows how unrealistic he could be.

The Austrian cavalry had started the French Revolutionary Wars as completely dominant over their French counterparts. As the war continued, their advantage waned. By 1801, they still believed themselves to be the best horsemen in Europe, but they were in for a shock four years later. While the Austrians' tactics and training remained stagnant, their French counterparts were creating cavalry that could function *en masse*. The majority of the Austrian cavalry was parceled out in 'penny packets' to the various infantry formations, which led to occasion after occasion where they would be thrown over by superior enemy numbers at the point of attack. Individually their cuirassiers, dragoons, *chevau-légers* and uhlans (lancers) were still good, but coordination was all but nonexistent.

While major efforts were being made to meet the supply and tactical needs of the Austrian army, scant attention had been given to its strategic doctrines. Austria still fought her wars by trying to maneuver her opponent out of theoretically vital geographic objectives. The concept of annihilation was foreign to the expensive armies that Austria fielded. However, the French Revolution and its levies had changed the way that war would be waged. Austria was not ready to adapt, adhering to a belief in a cordon style of defense, with fortresses holding key points. These would act as rocks against which the enemy would dash himself, while the field army massed to strike a decisive blow. Austria would in turn take the enemy's strong points and achieve 'checkmate'. The problem with this thinking was that it had failed against Napoleon in the past. But Mack would not tolerate the cautious thinking coming out of Charles's camp.

One final consideration hampered the Austrians: in order to place their troops under an Austrian commander, the Russians insisted that the commander be of the appropriate royal stature. The Protestant Mack would never do, therefore Mack's army was nominally placed under Francis's younger brother Ferdinand. Ferdinand failed to grasp that he was a figurehead until late in the campaign, causing no small amount of friction between the two leaders.

Russia

The Russian army during the Napoleonic Wars owed its origins to Peter the Great. It had grown and matured under the Tsarina Elizabeth and had nearly wrecked Frederick the Great's army during the Seven Years War. Under Catherine the Great and her son Paul, there had been a number of reforms and counter-reforms, depending on the political winds. But throughout there was a history of almost unbroken successes. Only during the last stages of the wars of the French Revolution did the Russians suffer any serious reverses. These the Tsar and his nobility blamed on their allies, the British and Austrians, and by and large it was a fair assessment.

The army was a typical *ancien régime* army, organized upon the regimental basis. There was no standing formation above the regiment and regiments were switched from one brigade to another on a moment's notice. The *inhaber* or commanding officer rarely took to the field. The drudgery of command was left to his subordinate.

The life of the typical Russian soldier was brutal even by the standards of the time. He was beaten on a regular basis, and while this was not unusual in *ancien régime* armies, the capricious nature of it was. The junior officers were of the mind that the majority of the men were animals. The food of the day was vegetable soup, most often made with barley and cabbage. The dark bread was baked to a rock-like consistency. This was either ground up into a mush or those brave souls that still had most of their teeth could attempt to bite it.

The Russian army was conscripted. Notice was given to landowners to provide a certain number of men, and he would pick the required number of his serfs (slaves) to send to the army. The term of enlistment was so long that villagers often held funerals for the departing men. With this attitude, it is easy to see that a high degree of fatalism consumed the vitality of the army. The men complained little, compared to their French counterparts, and had a reputation for withstanding high casualties stoically. While Russian soldiers were brave, numerous chroniclers have said that this was more from a sheep-like willingness to follow their leaders than from *élan*.

The Russian artillery arm was greatly admired throughout Europe. Their guns were plentiful and packed a good punch. The artillerists would doggedly defend their pieces, in many cases to the death, rather then abandon them to the enemy. While fierce, the gunners lacked the skill needed to get the most out of their guns. On many occasions the French out-dueled the Russians even though they were often outnumbered by more then two to one.

Poor training caused a chronic problem. The senior officer corps was made up of the upper nobility from St Petersburg and Moscow. The line officers, however, were often ill-educated, under-trained men who were beyond their depth at command level. Only the best-trained troops could perform the maneuvers required to keep up with the French. This meant that the best units saw continual service in battle. The command of Bagration would see more combat than the standard line division. They always responded well, but it meant that it was always the pick of the army that was taking casualties. It was with this brave but flawed army that Kutusov took the field.

Prussia

The Prussian army of the Napoleonic Wars
was the direct descendant of Frederick the
Great's. Perhaps no army has been so
undeservedly maligned throughout history.
One is required to examine the motives and
perspectives of the authors of these attacks.

It has been said that the army generals
were extremely antiquated. While the senior
commanders and staff were old, this also
meant that they had a great deal of
experience. The commander, after the King,
was the Duke of Brunswick. He was a veteran
of the Seven Years War, where he had won a
number of spectacular victories over the
French. He had commanded the army during
Prussia's participation in the wars of the
French Revolution, 1792–95, and had
performed well, with the exception of the
Valmy campaign. His failure to perform
at Valmy was just possibly a result of a
well-placed bribe, rather then a lack of

The Duke of Brunswick. Nominal commander of the
Prussian army in 1806, he was forced to fight a war he
opposed. Mortally wounded at Auerstädt, he died at
Ottensen on 10 November 1806. (Hulton Getty)

military acumen, for when the Duke's estate
was catalogued following his death, a
number of the former crown jewels of France
were found. The Duke's biggest problem was
that he stood between the King and a
number of 'War Party' generals, who
resented his more prudent policies.

The army itself started the campaign
dispersed throughout Prussia. They gathered
slowly and were still assembling in 1806
when the French thunderclap fell on them.
The 200,000 men were well trained and
efficient. Such was their level of training that
only the French of the *Grande Armée* were
better. The structure of the army was similar
to every other *ancien régime* army. There was
no permanent structure above the regiment.
Units were brigaded together as befitted the
wishes of the wing commander.

The Prussian cavalry was considered by
many to be the best in Europe. Certainly
their mounts were of the highest quality,
and the troopers were brave and skilled in
personal combat. If they lacked anything, it
was the ability to coordinate multiple
squadron charges efficiently.

The infantry, which had won such high
renown during Frederick's early campaigns,
retained the impressive level of fire discipline
of their forebears. These battalions could
pour out a devastating level of fire, and
maintain this pace until their ammunition
ran out. This meant that when the French
met the Prussians in a stand-up firefight, as
history would verify, huge casualties could
be expected for both sides.

The Prussians, however, had a significant
disadvantage in their inability to match
up well against the French skirmishers.
This failure of tactical doctrine became a
decisive factor when Prussian line battalions
exposed in the open tried to exchange volleys
with skirmishers who were able to take
advantage of cover. When the Prussian
fusiliers had cover, such as in the woods
around Closwitz and Isserstadt, they gave
the French *tirailleurs* all they could handle.
But Prussian commanders did not exploit
villages or woods as defensive strongpoints,
instead preferring open ground to use the

musketry machines that their infantry battalions had become.

Another problem was Prussia's artillery arm, the majority of which used obsolete guns. They lacked much of the hitting power of the French pieces, weighed more, and therefore suffered in maneuverability. The French gunners were able time and again to outduel the Prussians and deprive the stolid Prussian infantry of critical artillery support.

Finally, we come to the much-maligned Prussian General Staff. While it is true that the Prussians lacked a modern General Staff, they were no different from any other *ancien régime* country such as Russia, Austria or Britain.

Prince Louis Ferdinand. The pride of the Prussian aristocracy, he commanded at Saalfeld and did not survive the experience. (Roger-Viollet)

Only the French command and control system had evolved its capabilities significantly since the Seven Years War. It is no coincidence that the other countries would basically adopt the Napoleonic model as the wars continued. The much-vaunted Prussian staff system of the nineteenth and twentieth centuries grew directly out of the failures of 1806, such that the later armies of Bismarck and the Kaiser could be said to trace a more direct lineage to Napoleon than to Frederick.

From Ulm to the Treaty of Tilsit

General Mack of Austria believed that the security of the Rhine front depended on closing off the gaps that led through the mountainous Black Forest area of southern Germany, where much of the 1796–97, 1799, and 1800 campaigns had been fought. He assumed that central Germany was out of play – in effect, neutral ground. The linchpin to his plan was the city of Ulm on the borders of Bavaria and Württemberg. By seizing and holding Ulm, he would maintain the position until General Kutusov arrived with the Russian reinforcements, whereupon the combined army would crush the upstart Corsican. At Ulm, the fortified position of the Michelsberg rose above the town, and Mack believed that this position was virtually impregnable. In this way, Mack predicated his defense upon a chimerical view of the situation.

The Ulm campaign

The first part of Mack's plan was to cross into Bavaria and, with the combined Austrian–Bavarian army, occupy the Ulm position. Francis sent his emissary to the Bavarian Elector to win him over by a combination of promises and threats. While the Elector's wife actively lobbied on the Habsburgs' behalf, a combination of Austrian blunders, popular sentiment, and Napoleon's offers of succor led to the Bavarians retreating to Würzburg and allying themselves to the French cause.

At almost the same moment that the Austrians were crossing into Bavaria, Napoleon was setting his army into motion. He correctly judged Mack's strategy and played up to Mack's preconceptions. While Mack took up a position at Ulm, the *Grande Armée* would feint at his front while making a

large wheeling motion and descending on his northern flank. That would interpose part of the French army between the Austrians and their supply line running through Munich.

On 25 September 1805, the 3rd and 6th Corps crossed the Rhine and moved on Stuttgart. Mack's army was strung out between Ulm and Augsburg as the trap began to close on the unsuspecting Austrians. Mack finally realized that he was

being outflanked on 3 October. Ordering garrison forces to deploy along the Danube, he waited with his main army in Ulm.

The first of Napoleon's hammer blows fell on 8 October. After crossing the Danube the day before, elements of the 5th Corps and Murat's cavalry reserve met a column under General Auffenberg hurrying to stop the French crossing to the right bank. As was to happen time and time again in this campaign, the Austrians were too late, and were in turn caught wrong-footed. In a running battle, Auffenberg's column was crushed at the Battle of Wertingen.

The following day, elements of Ney's corps forced the bridge at Gunzburg against determined opposition. The Austrians fought well, but again were defeated. Napoleon assumed that Mack would attempt to escape. In his mind the most logical route was for them to head south and meet up with a small force in the Tyrol under Archduke John. Therefore, Napoleon had most of his army swing south to head them off. He left Marshal Murat in charge of sweeping up the rearguard around Ulm. All forces were ordered south of the Danube. But Ney was still getting reports of significant activity north of the river. One of his divisions under General Dupont was up there, having been

The Battle of Elchingen. The abbey high on the hill was stormed while the battle raged on the flats below. (Roger-Viollet)

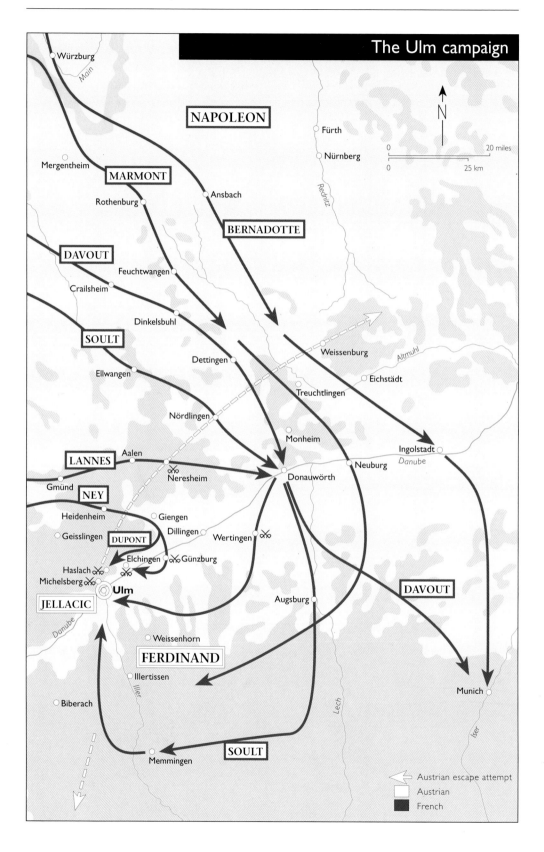

The Ulm campaign

General Dupont. Superb and aggressive performances at Jungingen and Friedland suggested Dupont was a coming man in the French army, but a craven defeat at Bailen in 1808 led to the greatest disgrace of any French general in the Napoleonic Wars. (Roger-Viollet)

from overwhelming the French right flank, diverting them into a wasteful attack on the French baggage. In all, not only did Dupont hold out against four-to-one odds, but he also inflicted five times the casualties, almost the equal of his entire force. The French were spent, no doubt, but they had put on an amazing performance. In the face of such Austrian numbers, with yet more Austrians that could be committed, Dupont beat a hasty retreat on the night of the battle. He had no desire to tempt fate twice, no matter how gallant his men.

On 12 October, the proverbial veil had fallen from Napoleon's eyes. Mack was still in Ulm and still in the trap. Mack, for his part, believing that his position was invulnerable, saw an opportunity to destroy the exposed French line of supply north of the Danube. After dithering and repeatedly changing his mind, he sent two columns out of Ulm on the afternoon of the 13th. One under General Riesch went towards Elchingen to secure the bridge there

Marshal Michael Ney. Although keen to display his worth before the Emperor, Ney's ill fortune was to shine outside his sight at Elchingen, but to be a scapegoat for failures at Jena and Eylau. Finally, at Friedland he was victorious while Napoleon was present. (Ann Ronan Picture Library)

ordered to move along the right bank to sweep up isolated units. Ney argued with Murat all day on the 10th that it was urgent to move his entire 6th Corps to the north of the river to support this increasingly isolated division. Nothing was resolved, and Dupont marched on.

Early on the morning of the following day, as he reached the suburbs of Ulm, Dupont discovered a horrifying sight: Mack and his army were still at Ulm and issuing forth to meet him. What transpired marked a clear demonstration of the superiority of the troops of the *Grande Armée* over their Habsburg opponents. In this desperate day-long battle, Dupont used the French superiority in street fighting to hold the village of Jungingen, counterattacking skillfully when the Austrians broke themselves on this strongpoint. The rest of Dupont's infantry barely managed to hold their left flank against the sluggish Austrians. His cavalry were defeated by their Austrian counterparts, but gallantly prevented them

Surrender at Ulm, by Thevenin. Although many of
the uniforms are anachronistic, this painting gives a
good idea of the scale of the surrender. (AKG London)

and prevent the French doubling back over
the river. The other column, under Werneck,
headed north with most of the heavy
artillery. After Riesch chased a small
detachment out of the town, he prepared his
defenses. According to Mack's calculations,
no French should have been in the
Elchingen area. What were they doing there?

Napoleon and Ney had hurried to
reestablish contact with the isolated Dupont.
The quickest route to this goal lay over the
bridges at Elchingen. On the morning of
14 October 1805, Ney led his men to a
position south of the Danube opposite
Elchingen. Having assaulted south over the
river at Gunzburg, Ney had to storm back
over it at Elchingen. The field was a partially
wooded flood plain, rising suddenly and
steeply to a hill town overlooking all. After
clearing the Austrian pickets with

This last defeat was too much for Archduke Ferdinand. He took most of the remaining Austrian cavalry and headed north, following after Werneck. He was going to escape, even if the foolish Mack would not. He rode through much of the night and out of this phase of the campaign to report to Vienna.

Following the victory at Elchingen, Napoleon released Murat to chase down Werneck. He finally caught up with him on the 16th at Neresheim and destroyed him in a running battle over the next two days. Meanwhile, Napoleon ordered the *coup de grâce*. As Ney, followed by part of Lannes' corps, approached the Austrian position on the Michelsberg on the afternoon of the 15th, Napoleon ordered an assault following a 30-minute bombardment. Stripped of their heavy guns a day earlier, the Austrians had no adequate response, and it turned out that the fortifications had yet to be completed because of sloth and the rains. Ney's 3rd Division under General Malher trudged up the muddy slopes. About 45 yards (40m) from the fortified lines they broke into a run. Amazingly, the 'unassailable position' of the Michelsberg was taken in the first try. Vicious hand-to-hand fighting left hundreds of dead strewn around the fortifications. By nightfall, the remainder of Mack's army was completely surrounded in the walled town of Ulm. With the loss of the Michelsberg their position was hopelessly compromised. Napoleon could shell them at his leisure from the heights.

Negotiations were opened on 17 October. Assured that the Russians could not come in time to his aid, and informed of Werneck's fate, Mack agreed to surrender on the morning of the 20th. As the remains of his army marched out of the city on that October morning, history witnessed one of Napoleon's most complete triumphs. Mack had lost over 60,000 of the 72,000 men with whom he had entered Bavaria. He had been no match for Napoleon's speed, and learned too late that no position is unassailable. Now Napoleon could face the Russians.

artillery, the corps advanced across the bridge. One regiment fought up through the town and took the abbey at the top with the bayonet. The rest of the division moved right across the low ground. They faced down the Austrian cavalry and scattered Riesch's infantry. Ney won the title of Duke of Elchingen for annihilating the enemy despite the imposing terrain. By evening on the 14th, communications had reopened and Ney was advancing towards Ulm, 6 miles (10km) away.

The Austerlitz campaign

After the capitulation of Mack's army on 20 October 1805, Napoleon took several days to gather the spoils of war and reorganize his army to head for the Russians under Kutusov. The latter's army had marched as far as the Inn river, on the borders of Austria and Bavaria, and then stopped. The march had been a terrible ordeal. Straggling and disease had cost the Russians about one-third of their men. In the past, much has been made of the scheduling problems caused by the Russian and Austrian use of the Julian and Gregorian calendars respectively, accounting for an 11-day difference. However, it appears that most of their difficulties arose from the false assumption that Napoleon could not bring his army to bear before the two armies of his opponents were able to combine.

When word reached Kutusov of the disaster at Ulm, he knew that the nature of the war had changed. He devised the

Prince Mikhail Kutusov. Immortalized as the ideal Russian commander in Tolstoy's *War and Peace,* in reality he was a very different man. Blind in one eye from a battle wound, well educated and a libertine, he conducted retreats with great skill, but seemed at a loss to do much else. (Hulton Getty)

obvious plan of falling back upon his supply lines and support. As he withdrew from the Inn river, Kutusov barely kept ahead of the rapidly marching French. He left rearguards who fought the French in a succession of skirmishes. At Amstetten, Murat rode too far ahead of his support and almost got himself killed. At Mariazell, Davout destroyed one of the last contingents of Austrians under General Merveldt.

The Russians faced the problem that their line of supply ran south from Brünn. This meant that to secure their retreat they had to move north of the Danube river. To do this, however, would expose the Austrian capital of Vienna. Understandably, the Habsburgs preferred that a defense of their capital be made, but after a show of making a stand, Kutusov slipped his army north of the river and positioned himself around Krems.

While this happened, Murat pushed ahead and found that the way to Vienna was open. With his cavalry he entered the city on 11 November. As Murat rode for the glory of capturing the enemy's palaces, to the north of the Danube dramatic events were unfolding. Napoleon had hoped to prevent the Russians from crossing the river and had sent a newly formed corps under Marshal Mortier over the river by a pontoon bridge to cut them off. The first division, led by General Gazan and Mortier himself, moved along the left bank. Following behind was another division under Dupont. Without any cavalry screen, Mortier did not know he was walking into a trap. As he spent the night encamped around the town of Dürrenstein, Kutusov had complete knowledge of his position and sent several columns around to the north to come into the rear of the Marshal while attacking at the same time to the front.

This plan worked, but the march through the freezing night took much longer than anticipated. Gazan's men fought fiercely most of the day against heavy odds. They were able to exploit the vineyards on the hillsides to their best advantage and were on the point of preparing a final push to break the troops to their front when the tardy

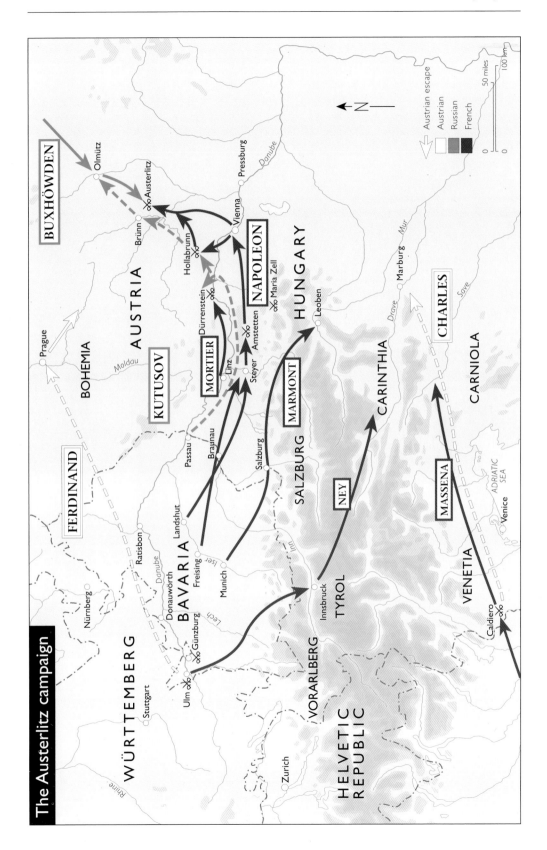

The Austerlitz campaign

Russian columns appeared in their rear. Mortier turned his men around and tried to punch his way out. Much of the fighting occurred in the streets of Dürrenstein. The men were running out of ammunition and were completely exhausted. Surrender seemed inevitable when the report of cannon coming from the west was heard. Dupont's men had force-marched and were launching bayonet attacks in the evening gloom. The Russians, now fearing they were the ones who were in danger of being surrounded, broke off the action and retreated into the hills. The French had barely avoided a disaster that would have wiped out the propaganda benefits of Ulm. Only the tenacity of the French soldiers, outnumbered five to one, had saved the day.

Breathing a sigh of relief, Napoleon looked for a way to transport his army to the north of the Danube. He had dispatched the 2nd and 6th Corps of Marmont and Ney to cover the Tyrol and the approaches to Vienna from the south, for both Archdukes Charles and John with armies from Italy and Hungary could have threatened his rear had he not done so. This still left him with the 1st, 3rd, 4th and 5th, most of the cavalry,

Joachim Murat. The dashing cavalry leader became a Prince of the Empire because of his marriage to Napoleon's sister Caroline. While extremely skilled in leading cavalry, his performance in independent command left something to be desired. (Ann Ronan Picture Library)

Prince Peter Bagration. As the fearless leader of the Russian avant-garde, he caused more problems for the French than any other Russian. (Roger-Viollet)

and Mortier's *ad hoc* corps to face the Russians. Napoleon found the answer to his problem when Lannes and Murat bluffed the guards of the Vienna bridges into believing that an armistice had been signed. While the Austrian guards were distracted by the glittering French marshals, some French grenadiers swiftly seized the bridge. This act of daring allowed the quick pursuit of the now fleeing Russians. Murat caught up with them at Hollabrünn.

It was here that the Russians turned the tables, for Bagration now bluffed Murat into signing a temporary armistice in preparation for a permanent peace. While Lannes fumed, both sides agreed to a four-hour warning before resuming combat. A message was sent to Napoleon, who was enraged and ordered a resumption of the war. The respite had given the cunning Kutusov time to get most of his army away. After the required four hours the

Napoleon at the chapel of St Anthony. He is viewing the progress of the annihilation of the allied left, sending in his reserves as needed from this position. (Roger-Viollet)

French attacked into the night's gloom. Only the light provided by the burning town of Schöngraben allowed the men to work their way through the vines of the fields in front of the Russian position. Receiving canister fire from the Russian guns that overlooked their approach, they pressed on despite the huge swaths cut through their ranks. As they reached the Russian position it gave way, yielding many prisoners. However, Prince Bagration, the rearguard commander, had done his job. He broke off the fight and saved most of his command while allowing the main army to escape against overwhelming odds.

Kutusov was able to retreat through Brünn and continue on to Olmütz, where he

Lieutenant General Buxhöwden. A man much more interested in his drink and prostitutes than in military tactics, he spent much of the Battle of Austerlitz drunk while presiding over a monumental disaster. (Roger-Viollet)

exhaustion, and cold. The allies also had the chance to catch Napoleon with his army spread out. Desire for a victory prevailed at allied headquarters – ultimately, the Tsar wanted to gain the glory of commanding the army that would destroy this champion of the French Revolution.

met up with the reinforcing army of General Buxhöwden, including the Tsar, on 24 November. The combined army, which included about 15,000 Austrians, would number around 72,000 men.

An allied conference was held to decide what was to be done. Kutusov argued for a continued retreat to draw the French further from their supply sources, and this, in retrospect, was exactly the strategy Napoleon feared. It had the obvious advantage for the allies that they would not have to face the French immediately in battle. Further, there was an increasing chance that the Prussians would throw in their lot with the allies. The alternative was to bring on battle. This had the attraction of avoiding a prolonged retreat in winter, which could produce terrible losses from hunger,

The Mamelukes were part of the Imperial Guard Cavalry that Napoleon unleashed on the Staré Vinohrady. Many of them had followed Napoleon from Egypt, but over the years they were often recruited from Paris 'toughs'. (Musee de l'armée, Paris)

Napoleon wished to lure the allies into a decisive battle. His supply line was stretched and, in addition, his intelligence sources told him that Prussia was preparing to enter the war. Finally, and most importantly, the news of the naval defeat at Trafalgar, combined with the rumors floating around Paris about the situation of the army, had caused another financial panic. The Emperor was always aware that he was only one defeat away from a coup that could topple his throne. Napoleon therefore decided to bait the allies into bringing on a battle. He made the appearance of weakness by asking for an

armistice and being unusually polite to emissaries. While doing this, he sent orders to Bernadotte to march on Brünn and he recalled Davout from Vienna.

By 1 December the trap was set. In a further sign of weakness, Napoleon withdrew from the powerful position of the Pratzen Heights and deliberately weakened his right flank to tempt the Russians to attack there. The allies gladly occupied the heights and made plans to turn the French right flank and place their army between Napoleon's army and his line of communication. What the Tsar and his advisers did not know was that Davout had marched his two divisions the 92 miles (150km) from Vienna and was falling into place on the French right. Davout's men brought Napoleon's army up to about the same strength as that of the allies.

The allies were not the only ones who thought the French were in a bad way. On the night of 28 November, a group of marshals were meeting in the Imperial Headquarters waiting for the return of the Emperor. Soult and Murat were convinced that they were in for a drubbing and wished to convince Napoleon to retreat. Knowing that they did not hold the ear of the Emperor like Lannes, they cajoled him into finally putting forward the idea. When Napoleon returned, Lannes pulled him aside and suggested a retreat. Napoleon had never before heard such words out of the fighting Marshal and asked him where he had got such an idea. 'It was the idea of all of us,' responded Lannes nobly. 'I will place my corps at your service sire, and it will perform as double its number,' said Soult, trying to squirm out of the responsibility, whereupon Lannes drew his sword at Soult and demanded a duel. Lannes vainly tried to obtain satisfaction over the next few days. When challenged on the morning of the battle, Soult responded that they had enough warm work ahead of them that day without a duel. This incident would be the cause of a feud between the two marshals for the rest of Lannes's life.

Napoleon's battle plan was to tempt most of the allies off the Pratzen Heights in an

effort to turn his weak right flank. He would then launch an attack up the center and break the enemy in two, after which he would roll up both flanks from the middle. The allied plan fell right into Napoleon's trap. Three columns were to descend from the heights and crush the French right and then turn to drive Napoleon against the Moravian hills.

On the night before the Battle of Austerlitz, Napoleon went on an inspection of the troops. As his soldiers recognized him, they lit his way by burning their bedstraw, which they bundled into torches. Soon the entire camp area was illuminated by the men coming to see their Emperor. Napoleon would call it the finest night of his life.

By 6 am the Russian and Austrian columns were on the march. The Austrian Weyrother, Tsar Alexander's Chief of Staff, had drawn up a detailed general plan the night before while Kutusov slept. Weyrother's timetable exceeded the capabilities of the army, and had not accounted for various columns crossing paths and becoming confused. Count Langeron had to stop his column to allow for the cavalry of General Liechtenstein to pass through to their assigned place. Ironically, this delay nearly upset Napoleon's plans.

As the allies came into the fields opposite the towns of Telnitz and Sokolnitz, Vandamme's and St Hilaire's divisions were massing at the foot of the Pratzen Heights, waiting for the signal to advance. Their position was hidden from above by thick fog which hung in the low ground.

At around 8 am the first allied column attacked the village of Telnitz. Defending the village was the 3rd Line regiment. After several assaults on the town, the French were expelled and retreated to the west of the Goldbach stream. Moments later a French brigade came up, as Davout arrived on the scene and immediately poured his men into battle. They launched a counterattack and once more regained Telnitz. They in turn were routed when coming out the other side of the village, attacked by Austrian hussars. The allies once more regained the village, but were prevented from advancing further

Nicolas-Jean de Dieu Soult. Called the
greatest maneuverer in Europe, he was a master in
training and bringing his corps to the battlefield.
Once there he took a less active role.
(Ann Ronan Picture Library)

by French artillery, which raked the exits
from the town.

Slightly to the north was the village of
Sokolnitz. A little time after the battle began
at Telnitz, the allied second column made its
first assault against the village of Sokolnitz
with its castle and walled pheasantry.
Defending here was the 26th Light, the
Tirailleurs du Po and the Tirailleurs Corses.
These were some of the best troops in the
Grande Armée. The fire from these battalions
battered the advancing column. General
Langeron, the column commander, decided
to blast them out of the village. He
unlimbered his guns and began a deadly
barrage. While this was going on, the third
column arrived and began an assault upon
the castle. Though they were taking
withering fire, the allies' superiority in
numbers told and the French light infantry
was expelled. They fell back, rallied and

counterattacked. This time it was the
Russians who were driven back. They in turn
rallied and once more threw out the French.
Then Friant's division came forward and
once more expelled the Russians.

For most of the rest of the battle, control
of Sokolnitz passed to and fro. After Friant's
attack, the French never completely lost
control of Sokolnitz. All was going according
to Napoleon's plan, for the more in the
balance the issue appeared upon the
Goldbach, the more reserves the allied
commanders would commit to that fight and
the less they would have elsewhere.

The last two weeks of the campaign had
been fought under overcast skies. On the
morning of 2 December 1805, the sun broke
through the clouds and began to burn off
the haze that covered the battlefield. At
8.30 am, Napoleon turned to Soult and asked
how long it would take for his men to reach
the top of the Pratzen Heights. 'Twenty
minutes, Sire.' 'Good,' replied the Emperor.
'Start your men off in a quarter of an hour.'

So it was that the 'Sun of Austerlitz' shone
down on St Hilaire's division as it began its
ascent. The Tsar spotted this movement and
asked what it could be. This wasn't supposed
to happen! Kutusov was ordered to send men
over to stop the French from seizing the
Pratzen and splitting the allied army in two.
The fourth allied column was on the march,
but could only feed in several battalions at a
time. They were no match for the finest line
division in the *Grande Armée*, but their
numbers were almost twice those of
St Hilaire. In some of the most desperate
fighting of the Napoleonic Wars, both sides
blasted away at each other. As one Russian
battalion gave way, another took its place.
Charge and countercharge led to melees in
which no prisoners were taken and the
wounded were bayoneted. After an hour of
the most savage fighting, the allied fourth
column effectively ceased to exist.

As all appeared lost for the allies, the
delayed portion of the second column
arrived on the scene. These were the troops
who had been separated from their main
body by errors in the marching order. They

were Austrians and inexperienced, but still they weighed in and attacked the tired French. Finally, the weight of numbers drove the French back off the heights. With ammunition getting scarce, retreat seemed the only way out. Instead the men fixed bayonets and charged. The battle had hung in the balance, but French *élan* carried the day. The Austrians fled down the back slope of the hill, and the French had broken the center.

Further to the north, Vandamme, with Soult's second division, launched an assault against the Staré Vinohrady, the summit of the northern portion of the Pratzen Heights. Two pockets of troops held out here. The first was dispatched when hit by three times their number after receiving point-blank

canister fire from guns that had been unlimbered in their face.

The second group was five battalions holding the Staré Vinohrady proper. These men were first tormented by the French light infantry tactics, then treated to a crushing series of short-range volleys from Vandamme's veteran soldiers. The Austrians were routed. The entirety of the Pratzen was in French hands. The Tsar had no reserves left to commit except his precious Imperial Guard. When it became clear to Napoleon that both ends of the Pratzen were in the hands of his men, he came forward from his headquarters of the morning, and advanced with his Guard to the top of the recently captured ridge. At the same time, he ordered Bernadotte's

battle, the first battalion of the 4th Line was crushed and its standard taken.

As Napoleon watched this from his new vantage point, he committed his Guard cavalry to counter the enemy's Guard. The field squadrons of his mounted Guard chasseurs and grenadiers slammed into the magnificent Russian cavalry. The French impetus was too much and the Russians were driven back on to their own Guard fusiliers, who had just re-formed. As they were on the verge of breaking, Constantine committed the last of his available reserve, the Guard Cossacks and the Chevalier Guard. These men swung the balance back in the Russian favor. Napoleon countered by sending in his personal guard of the service squadrons of Guard cavalry. They flew into the swirling melee, but the Russians still held a large numerical advantage.

As the fight hung in the balance, Bernadotte's 2nd Division under General Drouet finally made its appearance. Advancing on the flank of the Russians, they came forward in serried ranks, their battalions deployed in a chessboard fashion. This new support allowed the outnumbered French cavalry to fall behind the cover of their infantry in order to catch their breath, while maintaining pressure on the Russians with a galling fire. On the occasions where the Russians tried to follow, they met with a devastating crossfire and fell back. Given this development, the battle shifted in the French favor. When the Guard horse artillery rode up, unlimbered and poured canisters into the Russian Guard cavalry, the day was won. Falling back through the ranks of the Russian infantry, they disordered the Guard fusiliers just as the combined French Guard cavalry bore down on them. The result was a massacre. Sabering the fleeing Russians, the French Guard cavalry followed up for 0.25 mile (0.4km) until they called off the pursuit because of the exhaustion of their mounts. The victory was won – the only

1st Corps to advance and support the left of Vandamme's men.

With the loss of the Pratzen, the Grand Duke Constantine, the Tsar's brother and commander of the Russian Imperial Guard, launched a counterattack in an attempt to restore the situation. Vandamme's men had taken up a position in a vineyard just below the Staré Vinohrady. Sending forward his Guard fusiliers, Constantine saw these men push back the first battalion of bicorned soldiers, only to have the second French battalion drive back his men with a withering volley. As his men came back down the hill, the Grand Duke sent in several squadrons of his heavy Guard horse. They rode down the rows of vines and slammed into the weary infantry. In a brief question remaining was the escape of the allied army.

As Vandamme made his assault on the Staré Vinohrady, the action on the north side of the battlefield was heating up. The Russian cavalry column, under Prince Liechtenstein, was making its way towards the right flank of the French 5th Corps. Opposing them was General Kellerman and his division of light cavalry. Kellerman's command made up part of the cavalry reserve under Murat. Behind them was the infantry division under General Caffarelli. For an hour and a half, Kellerman fought a series of battles with the much more numerous enemy cavalry, besting them initially, then falling behind the infantry to regroup as their infantry comrades fired volley after volley into the increasingly disordered enemy ranks. Finally, Murat sent two cuirassier divisions to finish the job. These heavy cavalry, tremendously impressive in their polished steel breastplates and helmets, crashed into the remaining enemy cavalry, and sent it packing.

With the defeat of the Russian cavalry, Lannes could turn his attention to the defeat of the Russian avant-garde under Prince Bagration. All morning the brave and aggressive Russian Prince had been eager to make his attack, but no orders had come. Finally, as the situation in the center began to deteriorate, Bagration sent his men forward to seize the Santon, a small but prominent hill that jutted forth from the heights to the north. In an attempt to overlap Lannes's line to the north, Bagration sent a Jäger regiment around to the flank. There they met a murderous fire from the elite 17th Light and a large battery of former Austrian light guns that were placed upon the Santon. Reeling back, they fell behind their own artillery.

Lannes advanced in a counterattack only to be stopped by Russian artillery fire. Directing his guns to suppress the Russian artillery, the French corps artillery drove off the Russian guns after sustaining high losses. Once this was accomplished, Lannes could advance again, and with the help of his

supporting cavalry he eventually drove Bagration's men off the field. Lannes wanted to pursue the Russians but was held up by Murat, who held command on this part of the field. The failure to follow up aggressively would leave the Russians the nucleus of an army when it mustered a few days later.

The greatest spoils of the battle were won on the southern front. Napoleon now directed the unengaged units of his army to wheel to the south and crush the first three columns of the allied army. The brunt of the fighting fell once more on Soult's two divisions, St Hilaire's and Vandamme's. Descending the slope of the Pratzen, they crashed into the remains of the 3rd column. At the same time, Davout sent in his last reserves to take the two villages of Sokolnitz and Telnitz. The Russians who now held the castle at Sokolnitz were hit on two sides, by Davout's men from the west and St Hilaire's men from the north. Fighting heroically, most of the Russians perished rather than yield.

Count Langeron, commander of the 2nd column, could now see all was lost and made provision to get out with what he could. The commander of the avant-garde of the 1st column, General Kienmayer, did the same. The commander of the front, Buxhöwden, was evidently so drunk that he made a run for it, leaving little direction for his men.

To cover the withdrawal, Kienmayer deployed his best cavalry regiment, the O'Reilly chevau-légers. To counter, the dragoon division of General Beaumont, with six regiments, advanced. In a dramatic charge, the O'Reillys broke through five of the regiments. Only the sixth was able to force them to withdraw. Re-forming, the O'Reillys came on again against a line of stationary dragoons. The French cavalry peeled away, exposing a line of French Guard artillery, which belched fire and shot at the surprised Austrians. The gallant cavalry had had enough and broke. This now fed the panic that was spreading among the allies. Many dropped their weapons and ran for their lives. The path that many took was across frozen ponds that blocked their way to the south. As the men fled across the ponds, a combination of their weight and French artillery fire broke the ice and many men plunged into the freezing water. While these ponds were shallow, undoubtedly the shock killed many. With the ice breaking, those troops who were still north of the ponds threw down their weapons and, pleading for mercy, surrendered.

The allies had lost 25,000 men, 182 guns and 45 standards. The French had lost 8,500 men and one standard. While the numbers engaged had been about equal,

it is worth pointing out that Napoleon fought most of the battle with only two-thirds of his troops. The entire 1st Corps, Oudinot's grenadier division, Legrand's division of Soult's 4th Corps, and the Guard infantry had seen very little action, while the allies had left almost nothing uncommitted. Napoleon had many

Napoleon meets Francis I following Austerlitz. Francis was relieved to get off so lightly after such a defeat, but Napoleon had other foes in mind. (Hulton Getty)

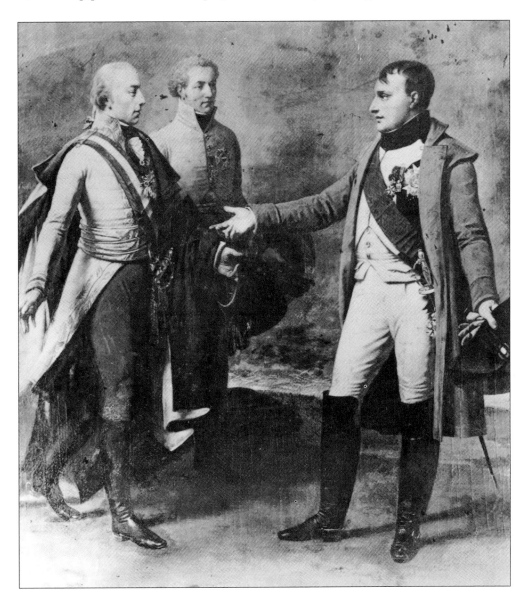

options left to him at the end of the day; Alexander had none. The battle had been won when Napoleon had lured the allies into the battle he had wanted.

Napoleon, in his address to the troops the following day, said that he was well pleased with them. Their hard work on the plains above Boulogne had paid off. They were superior in skill and training to their counterparts. Added to this, there was Napoleon himself – seldom has a general not only predicted the enemy's moves, but actually provoked them. Perhaps Tsar Alexander summed it up best: lamenting the defeat, he declared, 'We are babies in the hands of a giant.'

On 4 December 1805, the Austrians signed an armistice, and on the 27th, by the Treaty of Pressburg, they exited the war. The Russian army was allowed to withdraw to its homeland and the French army began to disengage from Moravia. Eventually they would set up in cantonments throughout southern Germany. Napoleon returned to Paris amid the triumph afforded a conquering hero.

With the formation of the Confederation of the Rhine, the role for the Holy Roman Emperor ceased to exist. Facing a *fait accompli*, the Emperor Francis II gave up his title and became Emperor Francis I of Austria-Hungary. The news of Austerlitz was said to have killed the British Prime Minister, William Pitt the Younger, Napoleon's arch-antagonist. The Sun of Austerlitz was shining on all Napoleon's realm.

Prussia joins the war, 1806

As 1806 arrived, there was little thought in the court of France of a war with Prussia. On the contrary, negotiations were continuing for a formal Franco-Prussian alliance. Napoleon had offered the much-prized Hanover to Prussia in exchange for the small provinces of Cleves, Berg, and Neufchatel. Additionally, Bavaria would swap Ansbach for part of Bayreuth. All these territorial changes would serve two purposes for France. They would consolidate the holdings of the two spheres of influence as well as alienate Great Britain from a potential ally. In fact, once Prussia occupied Hanover, Britain declared war on Prussia, although it can hardly be said that the conflict was prosecuted in any serious manner.

Napoleon continued to pursue the war against Britain and her allies, the greatest success coming with the removal of the

Queen Louisa of Mecklenburg. As Prussia's Queen, she became the focal point of those wishing war with France. She used every weapon at her disposal to defeat Napoleon. Her death in 1810 came before her country's resurrection. (Ann Ronan Picture Library)

Officers of the elite Prussian gendarmes cavalry regiment show their contempt by sharpening their swords on the steps of the French embassy (by Myrbach).

Bourbons in Naples and the installation of his brother Joseph on the vacated throne. While this was happening, however, more storm clouds were gathering. Prior to Austerlitz, Tsar Alexander had visited the court of Prussia and had fallen under the spell of the beautiful francophobe Queen Louisa. Making a pledge of mutual support in a melodramatic ceremony in the crypt of Frederick the Great, Russia and Prussia made plans to work in concert. The first result had been Prussia's tardy decision to exploit her position and enter the war on the side of the allies, just as Napoleon had reached his most extended point of the 1805 Austerlitz campaign.

Arriving at the Imperial headquarters just prior to the great battle, Haugwitz, the Prussian Foreign Minister, had been prepared to deliver the ultimatum that would bring Prussia into the war. Napoleon berated Haugwitz for hours and sent him away before the message could be officially delivered. When Napoleon next met Haugwitz on 15 December, the situation had changed significantly. Haugwitz meekly offered congratulations from the Prussian court to the recent victor. Napoleon quipped, 'It seems that there has been a change of address since the letter was penned.'

Prussia was caught between a rock and a hard place. Napoleon exploited her position by demanding the alliance and a break with Britain. While Prussia was handsomely compensated for the action, Queen Louisa and the 'War Party' were in a state of near apoplexy. Napoleon had triumphantly outmaneuvered them.

He was helped in no small measure by the 'Peace Party', which was led by the King, Haugwitz, and the Duke of Brunswick. They sought to obtain the best deal for Prussia while not risking her army. This prudent course had the disadvantage of having no appeal to the brash character of the Prussian nobility, who still regarded their army as the finest in the world. Louisa loathed the French Revolution and its minions and had been busy trying to gather allies for a renewed war effort against 'the Usurper'. The 'War Party' was made up of most of the General Staff, including Hohenlohe and Blücher, plus the young, dashing Prince Louis. They all relished the opportunity to attack and destroy the French.

Napoleon had been busy consolidating the gains of the last year and had formed the Confederation of the Rhine, which was an assembly of German states under the protection of France. This move threatened the Prussians, even though Napoleon had encouraged Prussia to take similar measures for the northern German states. Napoleon genuinely wanted peace at this stage of his career, and in the spring of 1806 he made strong overtures to Britain and Russia. The Russian ambassador had worked out a treaty that offered Russian withdrawal from the Ionian Isles in exchange for the withdrawal of French troops from Germany. This had every prospect of bringing about peace, but Queen Louisa had been haranguing her husband into opening negotiations with Russia for a renewal of hostilities.

The Prussians vacillated between committing for war or peace until word reached Berlin from the Russians that Napoleon had offered Hanover back to Britain. This was only partially true, for Napoleon had indeed floated the idea, but with the stipulation that suitable compensation be given Prussia in exchange. It is doubtful that this latter stipulation was passed on to the Prussians, but whatever the truth, the news tipped the balance in favor of the War Party. Russia and Prussia signed an agreement and prepared for war. The treaty Napoleon had signed with the Russian ambassador was repudiated and Russia began once more to mobilize.

As the summer wore on, Napoleon remained convinced that the peace would be maintained. He delayed call-up of the reserves until 6 September 1806. He believed that the Prussians would never commit the 'folly' of going to war against him, but took measures to secure himself against all eventualities. As late as 10 September, a full

month after Russia and Prussia had determined to go to war against the French, he wrote to Berthier that he expected peace.

After the Russians rejected the treaty, Napoleon began to take measures that would allow him to gather his army together quickly. The implications of the rejection of such a generous treaty could only mean one thing. Letters were sent to Prussia saying that Saxony must not be forced to join any confederation against her will. As this letter was going out, Prussia was doing just that to the reluctant Elector. Under threat of invasion, Saxony was instructed to ready its army to march with the Prussians against France.

The problem the Prussians faced during their one-month head start on Napoleon was the lack of any consensus on how to prosecute the war. For over a month the General Staff argued, and ultimately came to no final opinion. This weakness has to be placed squarely at the feet of the King, for had he taken charge and decided on any one of the alternatives presented, even the worst of them would have trumped indecision and turmoil.

By 18 September, Napoleon, after receiving many reports from his diplomats and spies, decided that war was inevitable. He dispatched orders to his various corps that were spread out all over southern Germany. Within days his army was on the march. He headed toward Würzburg where, headquartered in the Bishop's residence, he made his final plans for his campaign. After receiving the reports as to where the enemy was located, he initiated his plan to move through the Thuringerwald area of forest and hills and descend off the plateau into the valley of the Saale, thereby placing his army between the main Prussian force and Berlin. Furthermore, he wished to move with his usual speed, for he hoped to defeat the Prussians before the Russians could march to their support.

The Prussians assumed that the Russians under General Bennigsen would join up with their army by the beginning of November. Totally misjudging the speed with which Napoleon could react, the Prussians issued an ultimatum to Napoleon intended to

The opening moves

As the *Grande Armée* advanced, it moved in three parallel columns, each within one day's march of the other. The left column was made up of Lannes' 5th Corps and Augereau's 7th Corps. The middle column was headed up by Bernadotte's 1st Corps followed by Davout's 3rd Corps, both supported by cavalry. The right column consisted of Soult's 4th Corps, Ney's 6th Corps, and the Bavarians.

The first contacts occurred at Hof and Saalburg; at both places the French cavalry pushed back the Prussian screen. The following day, 9 October, Murat, heading up Bernadotte's light cavalry and the lead division of his infantry, attacked the Prussian rearguard at the town of Schleiz. With Napoleon on the field, Murat led a number of impetuous charges that required the infantry to extricate him. In the end, reserves arrived and drove the Prussians from the field. On the next day, Marshal Lannes came down the slope leading towards the town of Saalfeld. There waiting for him was a sizable force under the command of Prince Louis. The battle that followed demonstrated all the French tactical advantages in this campaign.

The contest opened with the 17th Light Infantry breaking out into skirmish formation opposite stiff combined arms opposition. While the French lights could not press the Prussians, their ability to use the terrain to the best advantage worked in their favor. It bought time for Lannes to send a column through dense woods to emerge half a mile (0.8km) away, thereby expanding the front. As more of his corps came up, Lannes was able to mass his troops in preparation for a coordinated assault. Using the ground to their advantage and massing quickly to assault key positions, Lannes's men were able to drive back the now outnumbered Prussians and Saxons. In a sharp battle the French overwhelmed their opponents, killing the Prince in the process. The French had taken 34 guns and four flags, and inflicted 1,700 casualties for a loss of fewer than 200. The victory would send

King Frederick William of Prussia. Crowned in 1797, he preferred a neutral policy with France until his Queen and the army's militants dragged him into war. (Ann Ronan Picture Library)

provoke war. He was given until 8 October to respond. Napoleon had arranged for signalling stations to be set on commanding ground throughout the territories he controlled, where flags or lights were used to pass messages. Because of this semaphore system he knew of the ultimatum's contents at once, but no official delivery could be made to the Emperor in Paris as he was already in the field preparing for his lightning stroke against the Prussians. The messenger finally caught up with him on 7 October after going by way of Paris. Napoleon's answer was to send the lead corps of his army over the border into Prussia on the morning of the 8th.

shock waves through the Prussian royal household. Not only had the pride of Prussia, Prince Louis, fallen, but the French were obviously able to deal with the Prussian army as they had the Austrians and Russians.

Napoleon's army swept up the right bank of the Saale, and the towns of Jena and Gera fell into their hands. On 13 October, the lead element of Davout's 3rd Corps entered Naumburg and captured a number of pontoon bridges over the Saale. The Prussians were hurriedly concentrating on the left bank of the river with the center of their forces around Weimar. Having

been beaten in two piecemeal engagements, Brunswick wished to meet the French threat massed.

Lannes's 5th Corps entered Jena on the morning of the 13th and soon crossed the river, climbed to the heights above the town and assembled on a sheltered plateau below

the village of Cospeda. Here his scouts reported that he was faced by 40,000–50,000 Prussians. Lannes sent a report to the Emperor and deployed his men to face any attack. Retreat doesn't seem to have entered his mind, for Lannes had total confidence in his men. On the evening of the 13th, Prussian Prince Hohenlohe began to move troops forward to the attack, but he canceled the assault, probably after being reminded of his role as a rearguard and not an attack wing.

Napoleon assumed that the Prussians had gathered an army on the heights above Jena for the purpose of cutting across his lines of communication should he advance upon Berlin. This was an entirely logical assumption and reflected what he would have done in the same situation. Napoleon felt the need to bring the Prussians to battle soon, for if too much of a delay occurred, the Russians under Bennigsen might arrive in the theater of war. He told Lannes to hold in place and quickly ordered Soult, Ney, the Guard infantry, and two divisions of heavy cavalry to force-march to Lannes's assistance. Once assembled, he would bring on a battle.

The orders to Marshal Bernadotte were to work in conjunction with Marshal Davout and move upon Dornburg and, from there, Apolda. The two marshals detested each other and Bernadotte chose to follow one part of the order, while deliberately ignoring the other. He did not feel he should act in a subordinate role to a junior officer, no matter what the Emperor's intentions were. His behavior would place Davout's corps in the greatest of peril, yet ironically bring eternal credit to the man he loathed.

Throughout the night Napoleon pushed his men as they passed through Jena, over the Saale and up the steep slope to the bridgehead on the Landgrafenberg plateau above. To get his cannon up the slope, caissons were double and even triple teamed. The Guard chopped down trees to widen the road where possible.

The death of Prince Louis (by Knotel). Separated from any escort, trying to rally his troops, Prince Louis was run through by a bold French cavalryman who did not even recognize him. (AKG London)

Even the Emperor dismounted and directed operations to get as many men as possible into position. As the men arrived, they took their place on the increasingly crowded field, some literally sleeping shoulder to shoulder. Tomorrow Napoleon would have enough men to fight a battle, for the danger of a desperately outnumbered Lannes being crushed had passed.

The Prussians had sprung to life after Saalfeld, and Brunswick had decided to restore equilibrium to the war by stealing a march on Napoleon in order to get his army between Berlin and the French. He decided to force-march towards Magdeburg, where he would be able to join up with the command of the Duke of Württemberg, which was at Halle. His plan was to leave a blocking force under General Hohenlohe, swing behind that force,

Prince Hohenlohe-Ingelfingen. Drubbed at Jena, he later surrendered humiliatingly at Prenzlau. (Roger-Viollet)

and make an end run through Auerstädt and up the river towards Halle and Magdeburg. The plan might have worked but for two things: the aggression of Hohenlohe and the heroics of Davout and the 3rd Corps.

Jena

The dawn of 14 October 1806 was very foggy; men claimed that they could not see 30 feet (10m) in front of them. While Napoleon was aware of the Prussians' position from the previous evening's reconnaissance, their exact alignment remained a mystery. What was needed was room to deploy his army as it hurried up throughout the day. This could be achieved only by driving the enemy out of their positions around Lutzeroda and Closewitz. Napoleon's main battle plan seems to have been to separate the Prussians from their

anchored position on the cliffs above the Saale river. Once the Prussians had been unhinged from this position, the French could use their superior ability to exploit the terrain.

Towards that end, at about 7.30 am, Napoleon ordered the 17th Light of Lannes's 5th Corps to the advance. They moved through the fog and opened fire blindly on the position in front of them. As they had advanced, they had approached slightly at an oblique, which exposed their left flank to deadly fire from part of von Zezschwitz's Saxon division. Fortunately for the light infantry, their supporting light cannon had been wheeled up to short-range canister position and poured in devastating salvoes. The Saxons fell back, which relieved the pressure.

As it became clear that this was quickly developing into a serious battle, General Tauentzien sent reports to his commander, General Hohenlohe. After initially dismissing Tauentzien's fears, Hohenlohe was convinced by the increasing level of noise of the battle that this was much more than a French reconnaissance in force. He now made the critical decision of the day. Rather then attempting to break off the action and withdrawing in accordance with his rearguard orders, Hohenlohe decided to counterattack and throw the French off the Landgrafenberg plateau.

It was now about 8.30 am and the fog, while still thick, had lessened to the extent that the Prussian army's position was coming into view. The advanced guard under Tauentzien held this area of the battlefield. These were the best light troops in the Prussian army. Lannes launched an attack that slowly cleared the Closwitz woods and unhinged the Prussian line. Several counterattacks were made by the troops Hohenlohe fed forward, but these were repelled by the fresh troops Lannes was also placing into the line. Not believing in a strongpoint doctrine that would have allowed them to anchor in a village, the Prussians were left with no other option but to fall back and realign their battle front

in a north–south axis, so as not to be outflanked.

As soon as the first shots had been fired, a message was sent to General Holtzendorff to support the Prussian effort by marching to the battlefield from his position above Dornburg. This he did, and arrived almost to upset the French day. As the Prussians and Saxons fell back to their new position beyond Vierzehnheiligen and Krippendorf, Marshal Soult was able to send his lead division around Lannes's right flank. It swung into the open ground beyond the woods above Closwitz. Here Holtzendorff appeared. His column consisted of a combined-arms force that included some of the finest cavalry in the world.

As the fog lifted, Holtzendorff launched his attack to break through to the main army. He had the misfortune to have run into perhaps the finest line division in the world, St Hilaire's. The cavalry made their charge and instead of following the standard infantry tactical procedure of forming square to meet cavalry attacks, St Hilaire, with both of his flanks protected by two villages, kept his infantry in line to deliver a volley. With no way to envelop the French line, the cavalry attack fell apart. The Saxons and Prussians formed up and tried again, but with similar results. Soult now released his cavalry against the disordered and blown enemy cavalry and put it to rout. The French infantry subsequently advanced and put the Prussian supporting infantry to flight. This work done, the division formed up and turned to march back into the main battle some time after 11.30 am.

At about 10 am, the situation had stabilized around Vierzehnheiligen. The French were waiting for reserves to come up and the Prussians were recovering their breath, covered by fresh reserves of cavalry. All night Marshal Ney had been pushing the lead element of his corps to arrive at the battlefield in good time. Ney had missed Austerlitz and had never performed in front of Napoleon. He was anxious to correct this shortcoming and make a dramatic difference in the battle. The lead element of the

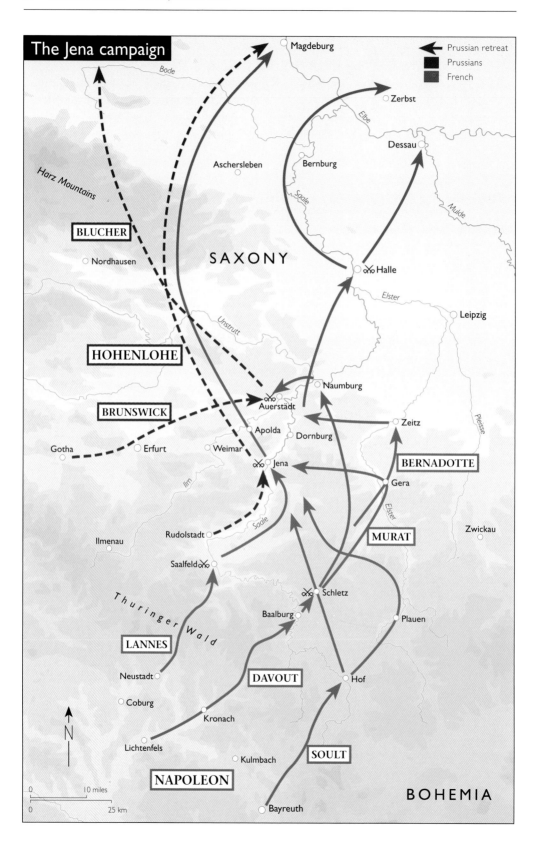

The Jena campaign

Prussian retreat
Prussians
French

Bode

Magdeburg

Zerbst

Elbe

Ascharsleben

Bernburg

Dessau

Saale

Mulde

Harz Mountains

BLUCHER

Nordhausen

SAXONY

Halle

Elster

Leipzig

Unstrutt

HOHENLOHE

Naumburg

BRUNSWICK

Auerstädt

Zeitz

Pleisse

Gotha

Erfurt

Weimar

Apolda

Dornburg

BERNADOTTE

Jena

Gera

Ilm

Zwickau

Rudolstadt

Saale

MURAT

Ilmenau

Saalfeld

Thuringer Wald

Schletz

Elster

Baalburg

Plauen

LANNES

Neustadt

Coburg

DAVOUT

Hof

Kronach

Lichtenfels

Kulmbach

SOULT

N

NAPOLEON

BOHEMIA

0   10 miles

Bayreuth

0   25 km

6th Corps pushed its way through a gap in the line, led personally by the red-haired Marshal. He launched an impetuous attack with just his lead infantry regiment supported by his two light cavalry regiments. The first cavalry regiment, the 10th Chasseurs, moved out of the woods and into the open, and overran a 30-gun battery. They were soon under attack from two Prussian cavalry regiments, one cuirassier and one dragoon.

Ney's second cavalry unit, the 3rd Hussars, fell upon the flank of the Prussians. A swirling melee ensued with the French having the worst of it. It was when several squadrons of Saxon dragoons joined

Napoleon in the Battle of Jena (by Vernet). Eager for battle, the Guard asked Napoleon to be committed, but he did not need them that day. (AKG London)

in that the French broke and fled to the rear. The German allies in turn charged and quickly overthrew the hapless infantry. A gap developed in the center of Napoleon's line and the crisis of the battle from the French viewpoint had arrived. Napoleon was much annoyed by Ney's rash decision, but reacted calmly to the situation. The Prussian cavalry had broken through the center and were threatening to roll up the line by wheeling to their left. Ney's remaining cavalry rallied and were still having the worse of it when the corps cavalry of Lannes charged into the fray, slowly driving back the Prussians.

While French quick thinking had averted a disaster, Napoleon had little fresh cavalry on the field. This meant that the Prussians could not be pushed until either more cavalry came up or artillery blew open a hole. Napoleon therefore began to assemble a massed battery of his Guard artillery and some of Lannes's guns in order to blast his way through Hohenlohe's line.

Around 11 am, Hohenlohe ordered an attack to retake Vierzehnheiligen. General Grawert sent forward the infantry of his column to assault the village. The French skirmishers of the 21st Light poured deadly fire into the massed infantry formations, but had to give way when Grawert brought up cavalry to outflank and surround the town. The Prussians seized the village, and were preparing to come out into the open on the other side when they spotted the massed guns of Napoleon. Seeing that they could not go forward and having no desire to defend the town, they set it ablaze and fell back.

The French countered by sending Gazan's brigade of Lannes's 5th Corps around the north of the village. They were met by Prussian and Saxon cavalry and driven back in confusion. Again the Prussian follow-up was stopped, this time by the battery supported by the newly arrived heavy cavalry under d'Hautpoul.

To the south of Vierzehnheiligen lay the village of Isserstadt, and there was a large wood just to the east. Since 10 am the French of Desjardin's division of Augereau's 7th Corps had been attempting to seize the village. Three times it had changed hands. Each time the French were able to keep a toehold in the woods because of their superior ability to skirmish. Any attempt to push the attack, however, was stopped by the two Saxon brigades and supporting cavalry arrayed to the south and west of Isserstadt.

A stalemate ensued, but by 12.30 pm the situation was looking grim for the Prussians. Fresh French units were pouring on to the battlefield. Heudelet's division of the 7th Corps was coming up from the south. The 2nd and 3rd Divisions of Soult's 4th Corps were moving to a reserve position behind the French center, and perhaps more telling, St Hilaire's division had swung into a position extending the French line further to the north, threatening to envelop the Prussian left. Napoleon had concentrated his artillery fire against the center of the Prussian line opposite Vierzehnheiligen.

Hohenlohe had few options left. His line was fully committed, with the exception of Tauentzien, who had rallied his men to take up a reserve position behind the center-left of the main line. He had sent word for General Ruchel to march from Weimar that morning, but as yet there was no sign of him. Napoleon kept up pressure everywhere along the line, while pounding the center. Finally, the pressure was too much and the decimated battalions began an orderly withdrawal. It was now that Napoleon gave the order to Marshal Murat to unleash his reserve cavalry. Eleven regiments passed through the gap between Vierzehnheiligen and the Isserstadt woods and plunged into the retreating enemy. This was too much for the Prussians and the center snapped like a dry twig.

The order passed down the French battle line to advance all along the front, and the result was repeated everywhere except on the right flank, where the Saxons were mostly unaware of the disaster befalling their allies. The remaining cavalry of the center and left tried to slow down the French, but they were swept back in the tide of retreating infantry. Only Tauentzien remained steady. His troops acted as a breakwater that their routed compatriots could rally behind. Although gallant, they did not last long, however. Hopelessly outnumbered and receiving a terrific pounding by the French artillery, they too gave way. What remained of the organized cavalry fell back trying to cover the retreat.

In the south, the two Saxon brigades held on grimly. They had lost almost all of their cavalry support and were now being assaulted by the entirety of Augereau's corps. To make matters worse, several regiments of French dragoons had peeled off the pursuit in the north and had come to harass these helpless heroes. Having no option but to form squares in the face of the enemy cavalry, they were systematically pounded by the 7th Corps batteries. For almost an hour they had huge holes ploughed through their ranks until sanity prevailed and the formations surrendered. Several of the battalions had taken advantage of the terrain to make an escape, only to be captured later that night.

While this was taking place, Ruchel had at last arrived at Kappelendorf. Here he formed up his 15,000 men and began an advance. Kappelendorf had a fortified château that would have been a formidable obstacle in the path of the French pursuit, but again Prussian doctrine prevented them from occupying it. As Ruchel moved up the slope past his fleeing comrades, he was first assaulted by the pursuing French cavalry. These charges his men were able to fend off, but it gave time for more of the French army to close in. As the cavalry withdrew, six French batteries bombarded Ruchel's men. Spearheaded by Lannes's and Ney's men, the French infantry came on. In their opening volley, Ruchel went down with a grievous wound. Napoleon's men would not be denied. The massed bands struck up 'Victory is Ours' and with a shout the French charged. It was over in the blink of an eye. The Prussians had had enough and broke and ran. Once more Murat launched his cavalry into a pitiless chase.

As the sun set on this gloomy October day, the French advanced guard rounded up the last of any organized opposition. Of the 54,000 men with whom Hohenlohe and Ruchel started the day, over 20,000 were lost,

in addition to 30 standards and 300 guns. These losses compared to about 6,000 of the French. While this disparity shows the magnitude of the victory, almost 14,000 of the Prussians lost were captured, making the killed and wounded almost equal on both sides. This was a testament to the firepower of the Prussians. Napoleon was triumphant, for he had crushed the main Prussian army, or so he thought. It was only late in the evening that he received his report from Marshal Davout. Looking up from the message, he told his assembled generals and marshals, 'Davout has had a rough time of it and Bernadotte has behaved badly.'

Auerstädt

On the night of 13 October 1806, Marshal Davout received his orders for the next day at his headquarters in Naumburg. He was to move on Apolda by the road of his choice. Similar orders were given to Marshal Bernadotte. This, Napoleon conjectured,

Prince-Field Marshal Blücher. A general at the time of Auerstädt, he heroically but foolishly led his cavalry against the French during the battle. A staunch member of the 'War Party', he surrendered near Lübeck – a stinging memory that fed his francophobia. He obtained his revenge in the 1814 and 1815 campaigns. (Hulton Getty)

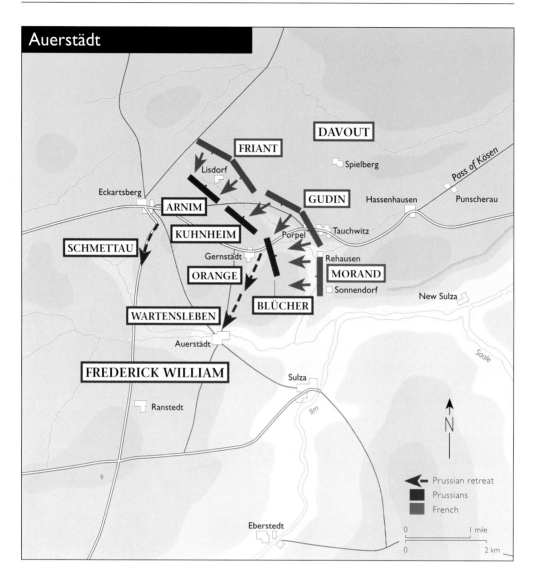

Auerstädt

DAVOUT

FRIANT

Lisdorf

Spielberg

Pass of Kösen

Eckartsberg

ARNIM

GUDIN

Hassenhausen

Punscherau

KUHNHEIM

Porpel

Tauchwitz

SCHMETTAU

Gernstädt

Rehausen

ORANGE

MORAND

Sonnendorf

New Sulza

BLÜCHER

WARTENSLEBEN

Auerstädt

Saale

FREDERICK WILLIAM

Sulza

Ranstedt

Ilm

N

Prussian retreat

Prussians

French

Eberstedt

0   1 mile

0   2 km

would allow both corps to fall on the Prussian rear. Davout dispatched orders for Morand's division to come up through the night so as to be able to support his other two 3rd Corps divisions under Friant and Gudin. Bernadotte chose to ignore the second part of the order to support Davout and marched his corps out of the action towards Dornburg. Bernadotte had hated Davout ever since 1799, when Napoleon asked Davout to spy on him and Davout had helped expose a conspiracy to overthrow Bonaparte. Lacking absolute proof, Napoleon pardoned Bernadotte, but the Gascon had never forgiven Davout. And now Bernadotte

saw no reason to subordinate himself to a younger man whom he outranked.

At 4 am on the 14th, the 3rd Corps scouting party ran into a large Prussian cavalry force in the village of Poppel. They scurried back to the protection of the leading infantry elements of Gudin's division, who quickly formed into a square. They had just come up the steep slope rising from the Saale river. They were approaching the village of Hassenhausen when the cavalry under General Blücher deployed between them and the village. Some French skirmishers had got into Hassenhausen just before Blücher's troops arrived and now came out and chased off Blücher's supporting cavalry battery, taking half the guns in the process. Stripped of this artillery support, Blücher launched several furious attacks upon the French squares. The heavy fog added to the confusion, but the crack French troops held firm and delivered deadly salvoes, both from their muskets and from the cannon that had been deployed at the corners of the squares. Blücher brought up more cavalry and another battery, which he deployed near the town of Speilburg.

Marshal Davout, who had been on the field since the opening moments of the action, rode from square to square to encourage his troops. After repeated attacks, the Prussian cavalry had had enough and broke fleeing from the battle. Blücher had a

The Prussian command decapitated (by Knotel). The mortally wounded Duke of Brunswick is led from the field. (AKG London)

horse shot out from under him, which in addition to the fog made rallying any of his cavalry problematic. The lull in the action allowed the rest of Gudin's division to arrive and deploy. Coming right behind them were the lead elements of Friant's *fantassins* (infantry).

As the fog lifted, Davout was able to see that it was much more than an isolated contingent that had attacked him. There spread before him was the main Prussian army. The largest contingents were deploying on the plain on either side of the village of Poppel. The King and the Duke of Brunswick had come up with Schmettau's division and had deployed it to the north of Poppel, but had waited to bring the division of Wartensleben into position south of the town to make a coordinated attack. This attack aimed to sweep aside the isolated force and allow the army to continue its retreat to Magdeburg.

This delay gave Friant a chance to arrive on the field, and after deploying he moved towards Spielburg in an attempt to outflank the Prussian line from the north. They overran the battery that had been dealing out death to Gudin's squares and swung their line to face south. At this same time, Davout broke Gudin's infantry out of square and formed a line extending north from Hassenhausen to meet the threat of Schmettau. Both sides closed and began a deadly firefight. Schmettau went down with two wounds and his line faltered.

To the south, things were going much better for the Prussians, directly under the command of Brunswick. They had maneuvered to a position south of the village of Hassenhausen and were on the verge of turning the flank. All that stood between them and the capture of the key town was the 85th Line. A withering fire was poured into the outnumbered Frenchmen and, when a cavalry charge came crashing upon them, the line gave way.

Davout had anticipated that the 85th could not hold out much longer and sent another regiment over to succor them. The 12th Line pulled up alongside the

retreating 85th and released a volley into the pursuing cavalry. The effect was to send them reeling back. The 85th rallied and formed square. The French position could have given way at any moment, and Brunswick was hurrying up two elite grenadier battalions to overturn the French. It was at this moment that a musket ball passed through both of his eyes, making him *hors de combat*. Ultimately, Brunswick succumbed to this wound on 10 November.

French marksmanship had decapitated the Prussian army. Schmettau was down, Brunswick was mortally wounded and Wartensleben had just been knocked senseless when his horse had been shot out from under him. The King was in charge, but seemed incapable of giving orders. The army command fell to the aged General Mollendorf, who proceeded to get himself captured. As a result, with no central command, the Prussians were incapable of getting off another coordinated attack, while the French under Davout were able to respond rapidly to each slow-developing threat.

Despite the dramatic change of fortune, the Prussians were able to exert tremendous pressure on the French holding Hassenhausen. Friant was attacking aggressively in the north, but just as Schmettau's right flank gave way, a new division under the Prince of Orange came rolling up to counterattack. Once more the two sides leveled crushing volleys against each other. It was now 10 am and Morand arrived on the field with his division. It fell into line, extending the left flank from Hassenhausen to the steep slopes falling down to the Saale.

By 10.30 am the Prussian cavalry of the reserve, along with the few remains of Blücher's command, deployed opposite Morand's infantry. Taking command, Prince William led the finest cavalry of Prussia up the slope towards Morand's men. Infantry fire out of the squares, along with the close-range canister, emptied many saddles including Prince William's. As if by a prearranged signal, the Prussian line gave way. The cavalry went streaming back toward Auerstädt. The infantry fell back, leaving their supporting batteries to their fates; most were captured.

Prince Henry made a last counterattack with several grenadier battalions. A heroic assault took the town of Poppel, but as the attack reached the apogee of its success, the Prince was mortally wounded. Once more the commanding officer of a wing went down. Void of any instructions and facing the talented commander General Morand, the bewildered grenadiers were enfiladed and forced back after a vicious fight. The King gave the order for the Guard to cover the retreat and for the army to break off. One rearguard was placed on the high point of this section of the field, the Sonnenberg; the other was left to contest the retreat route towards Eckartsberg.

French General Debilly, leading his brigade in the assault on the Sonnenberg, overthrew the position and captured many Prussians in the process. During this attack, Debilly was killed, the only French general officer casualty. This is contrasted with the devastating officer casualties taken by the Prussians, which can again be traced back in part to the decisive French superiority in skirmishing.

To the north, Friant led his exhausted men on the assault up the Eckartsberg hill. The disciplined Prussian infantry remained willing to stand and deliver deadly volleys. The French responded by breaking their lead battalions into skirmish order and working their way up through the woods. Taking cover, they sniped at the exposed Germans and eventually wore them away to the point that they broke. Those who headed for Auerstädt fell in with the mass of panicked troops who represented what was left of Prussia's finest. Those who went to the Eckartsberg were gathered up by the French light cavalry, who had swept around the northern flank to cut them off.

Jean-Baptiste Bernadotte. Despite his disloyalty and general incompetence during the Empire, he would be chosen as Sweden's Crown Prince and succeed to that country's throne. (Ann Ronan Picture Library)

The only remaining Prussian troops in good order on the field were a handful of grenadier battalions and the Guard. These men gave ground slowly, finally falling in with the remainder of the main army. Davout's men followed till they were sure of the result, whereupon they fell down from exhaustion. Davout was to occupy the castle in Auerstädt that evening and dine at the table so recently used by the King of Prussia and his high command. He had lost a third of his men, but the devastation was complete for his opposition. The King of Prussia had lost over 100 guns and between 10,000 and 15,000 men.

Aftermath

On the night of the twin battles, Napoleon assessed the situation. Davout was victorious, but exhausted for the moment. The lead elements of his army were in Weimar. Bernadotte was in Apolda. He had sent a message that his arrival in Apolda had saved Davout – a statement that was hardly justified by the facts.

Bernadotte: what should he do about him? Orders were given to arrest him in preparation for arraigning him for a court-martial. No sooner had these been issued than Napoleon countermanded them. Bernadotte was, after all, married to his former fiancée, who was the sister of his brother's wife. This would cause no end of domestic trouble to the Emperor. Better for Napoleon to give Bernadotte one more chance for now, while leaving his options open.

After getting reports of the day's actions, Bernadotte considered the position in which his pride had placed him. He had conspired against Napoleon several times in the past, on every occasion receiving a pardon upon discovery. But there was an end to every man's patience. He felt he would have to redeem himself, and looked for an opportunity to do so.

On receiving his intelligence, Napoleon issued orders for the pursuit to commence the following morning. The process was delayed because most of his men had force-marched to the battlefields and it took time to decipher the many reports that were coming in. Even with the delay, the pursuit that followed after Jena–Auerstädt was so devastating that one would have to go back to the days of the Mongols to find its equivalent.

Leading this hunt was the vainglorious Prince-Marshal Murat. He was in his element now. His cavalry would chase down Prussian formations with an intoxicating ruthlessness. Over the next week, his command would capture as many men as the combined Prussian losses of the twin battles. While Murat was chief in this gathering up of the straggling army, the infantry corps were doing their share moving up the Saale towards Berlin. Between them and the capital was the column of the Duke of Württemberg stationed around Halle.

Napoleon, on the morrow of Jena, began to wean the Saxons away from the Prussian

alliance. He sent messages of friendship to the Saxon Elector, and as a prelude to formal negotiations released his Saxon prisoners after receiving an oath of loyalty. The Saxons soon switched sides and fought with Napoleon the following year.

On the morning of 17 October, the leading elements of Bernadotte's 1st Corps attacked the dragoons attached to the Duke's forces on the outskirts of Halle. Driving the Prussians back to a series of three bridges that passed over the Saale river and then pressing

Prussian prisoners (by Myrbach). Entire Prussian armies marched into captivity, something the Prussians remembered for more than a century. (Author's collection)

on through the city, the French met supporting enemy infantry who held the three bridges. Led by the divisional general Dupont, the hero of Jungingen and Dürrenstein, the French soldiers set up a crossfire upon the enemy troops who were holding a dike, which sat above the swampy ground guarding the only approach to the outer bridge. The 32nd Line and a battalion of the famed 9th Light rolled over the bridge and quickly seized the two inner bridges under fierce fire. A panic occurred inside the city and soon all Prussian opposition had either fled or surrendered.

Dupont followed up to find that the Prussian main position was on the heights to the south of the town. Unable to press the position until reserves came up, the 9th Light sent forward a skirmish line to harass them. As more of Bernadotte's men moved into Halle, Württemberg realized that if they moved out of the city to the east, they would block his line of retreat. He therefore began to shift his troops from the heights along the front of the

Napoleon before the tomb of Frederick the Great (by Camus). Napoleon removed Frederick's sword from the mausoleum, saying, 'I prefer this to twenty millions [in plunder].' (Roger-Viollet)

city towards the north. This left them exposed to flanking fire and vulnerable to attack, which is just what Bernadotte did.

Leading his men out of the medieval gate, Bernadotte plunged into the Prussian line, committing himself to the midst of the battle. Splitting the Prussian army in two, the jubilant Frenchmen ran down whole pockets of the fleeing enemy. In an engagement lasting about two hours, half the Prussians were casualties, while they inflicted very small losses in return. Bernadotte had a victory on the scale of Saalfeld and, more importantly, Napoleon's forgiveness. This was to be his finest day fighting for the French Empire.

Between now and early November, a series of Prussian units and garrisons were caught and surrounded, and surrendered. Hohenlohe was trying to take the main army towards Stettin, where he hoped to revictual and head east to join up with the approaching Russians. On 24 October, Napoleon entered Potsdam and visited the tomb of Frederick the Great. Entering the crypt with several marshals and generals, Napoleon said, 'Hats off, gentlemen, for if he [Frederick] were here now, we wouldn't be.' On the 25th, Davout's

men had the honor of a triumphal march through Berlin, rewarding them for their performance at Auerstädt. On the 27th, the great fortress of Magdeburg surrendered after a mere ten-day siege.

Napoleon just had time to play the part of benevolent conqueror – and he knew how to play it well. Napoleon, now headquartered in Berlin, had the Governor of Berlin, Prince Hatzfeld, arrested after intercepting a letter written by him incriminating him as a spy. Facing her husband's execution, the Prince's wife went to Napoleon to plead his case. She assured the Emperor that her husband was incapable of doing the things with which he was charged. Napoleon showed her the letter and asked if that was not indeed her husband's handwriting. One look by the distraught wife made her husband's guilt clear, and she broke down weeping. Napoleon said that if she threw the incriminating evidence into the fire nearby, then there would be nothing left on which to convict her husband. This she did, and her spouse was saved.

The main Prussian army under Hohenlohe continued to retreat north, with Murat and Lannes in hot pursuit. As they chased the Prussians, both Lannes and Murat sent messages to Napoleon claiming that the other was unsupportive and slow. The old feud was pushing both marshals to have their men perform herculean feats of marching. On 27 October, General Lasalle's and General Grouchy's cavalry crushed Hohenlohe's rearguard at Zehdenick, where Queen Louisa's regimental standard was captured. On the 28th, Murat and Lasalle surrounded the town and Hohenlohe surrendered.

Lasalle went on to Stettin and tricked the garrison into surrender. Here he demonstrated around the city and claimed to have an infantry corps coming up that would show no mercy should the Prussians not surrender immediately. The ruse worked and the Prussians marched out of the city,

only to find that they had given up to fewer than 500 cavalrymen.

Marshal Murat peeled off after the surrender at Prenzlau and joined with Bernadotte's and Soult's corps in following up Blücher. They finally caught up with him at Lübeck. The previous day his Swedish ally had lost 600 men to Bernadotte. Ironically, it was Bernadotte's treatment of these prisoners that earned him a reputation for generosity that years later won him the crown of Sweden. Blücher had occupied the independent city of Lübeck in hopes of continuing the war. The French cavalry, however, stormed the two main gates of the city. While Blücher escaped with about half his men, the remainder fought a desperate street-to-street melee until they were compelled to yield. With all hope lost, Blücher

French triumphal march through Berlin. The victory parade was to set the fashion for many others over the following century. (Hulton Getty)

surrendered the remainder of the army on the following day in the village of Ratgau.

The entire Prussian army was now lost with the exception of those garrisons that had been out of the theater of war in occupied Poland and East Prussia. General Lestoq commanded the only field force in the following campaign. Additionally, the cities of Danzig, Colberg, and Stralsund would hold out for most of the next year's campaign.

On 21 November, Napoleon issued his Berlin Decrees. These closed all the occupied ports to British ships, and all British goods seized were forfeit. This was the beginning of the Continental System, an economic form of warfare that often at times seemed on the verge of success, but would ultimately undermine Napoleon's regime.

Other fronts

As the main French army operated under the Emperor, events were happening on a global scale. While Napoleon made his march against Ulm, the main Austrian army under Archduke Charles squared off against Marshal Massena. Massena's role was to entertain Charles while Napoleon destroyed

Mack and took Vienna. Throughout the month of October, the two armies maneuvered to gain advantage. Finally, they faced each other on the battlefield of Caldiero, the site of Napoleon's only defeat in his first Italian campaign. Massena knew that if he was not aggressive, Charles might give him the slip and turn the tide in southern Germany. So he attacked. The French acquitted themselves well, but Charles had almost twice the troops and was able to repulse the main attack.

The reverse at Caldiero would be salvaged by Napoleon, for word of Mack's capitulation reached Charles and ended all thought of

offensive action. Withdrawing his army in an attempt to reach Vienna to forestall Napoleon, Charles was forced to fight a series of rearguard actions and was slowed by the coming of the Alpine winter. In the end, he was miles from helping the allied armies when they were crushed on the field of Austerlitz. Massena had put Venice under siege, and when the peace with Austria came (the Treaty of Pressburg), the 'jewel of the Adriatic' was incorporated into Napoleon's Kingdom of Northern Italy.

Massena was now directed south to conquer the Bourbon Kingdom of Naples. Queen Caroline had signed a treaty of neutrality with Napoleon, but renounced it as soon as he marched north out of Vienna. A force of 13,000 Russians under General Lacy had landed along with 7,000 British troops to support a Neapolitan invasion of northern Italy. When word reached this force of the defeat at Austerlitz, the Russians and British pulled out, leaving the Queen with no option but to abandon her southern Italian holdings and retreat to Sicily under the British fleet's protection. This departure allowed Napoleon to place his brother Joseph on the Neapolitan throne. He arrived in Naples on 15 February 1806. The city of Gaëta held out and required Massena to conduct a five-month siege.

Attempting to stir up a revolt in the southernmost province of Calabria, British General Stuart landed a force of 5,000 men. Joseph dispatched General Reynier with about an equal force to attack him. The action at Maida on 4 July 1806 resulted in the French being routed by the British. Stuart failed to pursue and in fact soon retreated back to the protection of Sicily when the fall of Gaëta released Massena's troops to move against him. Calabria remained in revolt and presaged the type of savage guerrilla fighting that would be seen in Spain.

When Napoleon signed the Treaty of Tilsit with Alexander in July 1807, Britain became convinced that the Danes were about to join the French. Despite Denmark's trying to follow a strictly neutral policy, the British

Retreat of the Prussians (by Knotel). (AKG London)

attacked without provocation. Copenhagen fell, but the captured Danish fleet was found to be in poor condition. This provocation was too much for the Danes. They allied with Napoleon and would stand by him until near the end. Britain was considered a pariah for her piratical behavior. In the same year, there was another example of it. In the Argentine, a British expedition tried to seize Buenos Aires, but had to surrender in a humiliating fashion. In Egypt, another small British army landed to try to take the country. It took Alexandria, but was ambushed in Rosetta and driven from the country. At the same time a British flotilla under Admiral Duckworth was repelled from the walls of Constantinople. British military policy during this time was a series of disasters. It would take Wellington's campaigns in Spain and Portugal to reverse Britain's fortunes and reputation.

It was in 1807 that Napoleon, demanding that Portugal cut off all trade with Britain, sent an army under General Junot to occupy the country and force adherence to the Continental System. Napoleon offered to split the country with Spain and as a result the armies of the two countries occupied Portugal in the latter part of the year. Junot marched into Lisbon on 30 November 1807. The much-prized Portuguese fleet had sailed to Brazil under British escort. Disappointed, Junot was still able to set up a government and temporarily close the ports to British trade. Napoleon had taken his first steps towards the Iberian war that would sap so much of France's strength.

The Polish campaign

Following the final capitulation of Blücher and Hohenlohe, Napoleon set his sights on the Russians. He called up fresh recruits from France as well as from his allies. He had discovered that his Spanish ally had been on the point of betraying him, only waiting for any reverse against the Prussians. This had not happened, so Napoleon required that 15,000 of Spain's best troops under de la Romana be sent to support his efforts in

northern Germany. They would serve the double purpose of supplying him troops and acting as *de facto* hostages.

The Emperor had sent General Sebastiani to Turkey in an effort to convince Selim III to go to war against Russia. Sebastiani had been successful and so Tsar Alexander now faced a second front. The Tsar had been slow to mobilize prior to this because he had thought that he was only acting in a supporting role to Prussia in this war. With the exception of 20,000 Prussians plus a few garrisons and the ineffectual secondary fronts of Sweden and Britain, Alexander's army was now going to have to face France alone.

Both sides now made a race for the best areas in which to winter and prepare for an anticipated spring campaign. The immediate focus was Warsaw. The Poles had risen up and celebrated the arrival of the French, seeing them as liberators. Napoleon had to play a careful balancing act, for while he was sympathetic to Poland's cause, openly embracing it could draw Austria back into the war as well as making peace with Russia impossible. His immediate answer was to strip Prussia of her Polish holdings and set up a Polish client state.

As Napoleon advanced, he had to contend with two conflicting needs. The first was to seize the left bank of the Vistula river and the second was to mop up the various garrisons left in his rear. This he did in a leapfrog fashion. Progress was slowed by the muddy roads resulting from a thaw. Murat advanced ahead of the corps of Davout, Lannes and Soult.

Bennigsen had decided that he risked being cut off from the supporting army of Buxhöwden, which was coming by way of Tilsit. He abandoned Warsaw and retreated to the right bank of the Vistula.

Murat entered Warsaw as the liberator on the evening of 28 November 1806. He held the city until Lannes and Davout arrived to support him. The town of Praga, opposite Warsaw, was taken, which gave the French a passage over the Vistula. Further downriver, Soult, Bessières, Augereau and Ney crossed with their corps.

The Russians were still holding the Bug river, which, along with the Wkra and Narew rivers, gave them a good defensive position. Napoleon was now heading to the front and ordered Murat to break the Bug line. On 10 December, Davout sent a division across and secured a bridgehead to the west of the confluence of the Wkra and Bug rivers.

The Wkra, which runs on a north–south axis, still presented a strong defensive position. On 20 December, Davout occupied the island that was formed by the junction of the Bug and Wkra. Marshal Kamenski had arrived in Pultusk on the night of 21 December to take command of the Russian army and ordered an offensive against the strung-out French army. The Russian advance was blunted at every turn and Kamenski paused to figure out his next move.

Davout was looking to force the Russian position. With Napoleon on the scene, he launched a nighttime river assault on the 24th. In an amazingly well coordinated attack, the Russians were driven back. Napoleon ordered an advance over the hastily built bridges and the Russians were driven back to the towns of Golymin and Pultusk. By this time, Augereau's and Murat's men were also over the Wkra. The muddy roads were so poor that it was virtually impossible to move artillery. The advancing French columns gathered up several Russian guns.

On Christmas night, Marshal Kamenski ordered a retreat and left the army, apparently suffering a mental breakdown. Bennigsen once more took over command and decided to stand at Pultusk. At 10 am on 26 December 1806, Lannes' corps drew up to the south of the Russian position on the high ground around Pultusk. His guns had not yet come up, but he ordered an attack anyway. The lay of the ground masked the fact that Lannes was badly outnumbered, for he was facing the main Russian army of 45,000 men. Lannes drove the outposts of the Russians back and then brought up his main attack columns. Claparede's division hurled itself against the Russian left, pushing back the Russian first line slowly.

It was beginning to snow and vision was becoming difficult. Wedell's leading brigade, who were in the center of Lannes's line, began to wheel to their right to fall upon the troops in front of Claparede. As they did so, Russian cavalry came charging out of the snow and fell upon their flank. Hand-to-hand fighting went on, with the Russians having the better of it until Wedell's second line came up and fell on to the flank of the cavalry. Eventually falling back, they left many sabered French behind.

Lannes's cavalry were committed now, but were surprised when the Russian cavalry opposite fell away to reveal a massed battery, which unloaded a crushing canister salvo. As the French cavalry streamed back to their lines to re-form, Claparede's men succeeded in driving back the first line in front of them, capturing their guns in the process. Coming to a deep ravine running in front of the Russian reserves, they made several attempts to cross, but each time they were driven back. Bennigsen then released his reserve, and the French right flank slowly fell back under overwhelming pressure.

General Bennigsen, Russian commander at Eylau and Friedland. A master of writing communiques, Bennigsen was always able to make his defeats appear like victories. (Hulton Getty)

While this action was going on, Lannes was leading Suchet's division against General Barclay de Tolly's column. Deployed in a wood on the Russian right, Barclay's men were a formidable force outnumbering Lannes's more than two to one on this portion of the field. The French came on in skirmish order, taking advantage of the cover afforded by the trees, but Barclay's men were every bit their match. Even the inspiration of Lannes and Suchet leading their men from the front was not enough to overcome the determination of the Russian *Jäger* and line units.

As the day darkened because of the season and a relentless snowstorm, things were near breaking point. The French had all their men committed to battle and ammunition was running low after four hours of combat. Runners were sent back to replenish the ammunition, but the whole line was under pressure and the main supply wagons had not been able to get to the front because of the muddy road. The center was being held by Lannes's artillery, which after finally coming up had been engaged in a furious counter-battery fire with three times its number of Russian batteries.

At noon, several miles away General d'Aultanne, temporarily commanding Gudin's division of Davout's corps, heard the heated artillery exchange. Abandoning his plans to camp for the night, he marched to the sound of the guns. At about 2.30 pm, his men fell upon the flank of Barclay's men. Falling back on to Bennigsen's center, Barclay's men rallied and plunged back into the battle. The 34th Line was now out of ammunition and gave way. This created a gap between Lannes and d'Aultanne into which poured 20 squadrons of Russian cavalry. In the snow they were able to sweep around both divisions largely undetected. However, cries went down the French line and units formed square to repel the attack. Fortunately for the French, the snow that had aided the breakthrough also obscured the squares from a severe pounding from the Russian artillery in the center. The Tsar's cavalry, after repeated charges against the formed French, fell back through the line.

With the exception of the woods, where fighting continued in a desultory fashion for another couple of hours, the battle was over. Lannes had lost about one-third of his number while inflicting slightly fewer casualties on his opponent. The following day Bennigsen resumed his retreat and Lannes's 5th Corps was too exhausted to follow up.

While the desperate battle was going on at Pultusk, several miles away at Golymin, General Gallitzen was fighting a heroic rearguard against odds as bad as Lannes was facing. Left to cover the retreat of the Russian right, he had one small column to face three divisions with supporting cavalry. Given his instructions by his superior General Doctorov, Gallitzen deployed his men around the town. He was fortunate that the area was surrounded by heavy woods and swampy ground. The only access for cavalry or artillery was by the few roads that led into the village. In the morning, Lasalle's cavalry and the two divisions of Augereau's corps attacked Gallitzen's position. The French cavalry was thrown back by the charge of three squadrons of Russian cuirassiers. The two divisions, lacking their artillery, dissolved into skirmisher attacks about noon after their initial attacks were repulsed.

About this time, Murat and Davout arrived. Davout sent Morand's division into the attack. He drove back the Russians, but their resistance stiffened as they found the safety of the houses of the town. In an attempt to scatter the Russian cavalry who were impeding the French assault, General Rapp, an aide-de-camp of the Emperor, led a charge of dragoons down the road leading into the town. The Russian cavalry stood to meet them as the French rumbled down the road towards them. Suddenly standing up from the reeds that flanked the road were Russian infantrymen, who delivered a withering volley. Many saddles were emptied and the riderless horses fled down the road along with the remainder of the routed dragoons. As night covered the land, Gallitzen was able to break off his men and follow his withdrawing army.

When he received the report of Golymin, Napoleon was dismayed, for this ended the chance to pin the Russians against the Narew river. As it was clear that the Russians had escaped his trap, Napoleon ordered his men into their winter camps the following day.

Both sides felt pleased with their position. Bennigsen told the Tsar that he had defeated Napoleon and 60,000 men at Pultusk. He received the high command of both his and Buxhöwden's army as a result. Things would have remained at the status quo, had it not been for the aggressive actions of Marshal Ney. Hoping to increase the forage area of his corps as well as put himself in a position to be the first corps to take Königsberg, he began to extend his corps. Bennigsen caught wind of this and thought it a perfect opportunity to crush an isolated French corps. He began his winter offensive on 10 January 1807. His first contact with Ney was on the 18th. This cavalry skirmish helped to alert Napoleon to the Russian movements. Napoleon formulated a plan to move the 3rd, 4th, and 7th Corps from the south and pin the Russians against the coast and the 1st and 6th Corps.

The Battle of Eylau (by Bovinet). The church at Eylau, the highwater mark of the Russian advance, still stands there, turned into a factory building by disrespectful Russians in the 1960s. (AKG London)

The operation was well under way when Napoleon's plans were captured and Bennigsen realized his danger. Ordering a retreat, he fell back first to a position around Allenstein and finally to Eylau. There were three sharp actions at Mohrungen, Bergfried and Hof; all were indecisive, yet forced the Russians back further. All the time Napoleon was hot on their heels. On 7 February, the Russians turned and fought Soult's corps for possession of Eylau. Both sides wanted to sleep in the meager shelter that the town afforded against the bitter cold. In a tough fight, Soult's men were finally able to shelter with cover over their heads. It is most probable that the first day's actions were brought about accidentally.

Eylau

As day broke on 8 February, Napoleon had on the field 44,500 men opposite Bennigsen's 67,000. Napoleon thought that he had Ney's 10,000 men coming on fast as well as Davout's 5,500. All he wanted to do was fix the enemy in place and watch his reinforcements turn both flanks. The Russians did not intend to stand by passively and be defeated. They opened the battle with a

terrific barrage by a grand battery of over
100 guns. This bombardment pulverized the
French center. The French, with less then half
the guns in action, responded in kind, but
were hampered because a driving snowstorm
was blowing straight into their faces.

Napoleon had Soult attack the northern
flank in an attempt to draw away troops from
the south, where Davout was coming up.
Soult advanced and the Russians responded
effectively. Soult soon recoiled to the safety
of the main line, having unquestionably got
the worst of it. By now the first of Davout's
divisions, under Friant, was deploying.
A large Russian cavalry contingent was sent
to attack them. This forced the French to
close up to meet the onslaught and the key
assault lost its impetus.

To relieve the pressure, the Emperor
sent forward Augereau's corps in an attack
on the Russian center. The men fought
against the driving storm and waded

The cavalry charge at Eylau. By committing his superb cavalry in mass, Napoleon regained the initiative. (Roger-Viollet)

The *Grénadiers a cheval* charge at Eylau. That Napoleon committed this regiment, the finest regiment of his Guard, showed his determination to reverse the tide of battle. (Roger-Viollet)

through 2 feet (0.6m) of snow. As they moved forward they drifted off track, exposing their flank to the line of the Russian barrage. Equally destructive was the fire of their own guns. The swirling snow had so blinded the gunners that they were firing at the last-known Russian position and it was into this line of fire that Augereau's men wandered. As they were hit from all sides, confusion reigned. Bennigsen seized the opportunity and sent a cavalry division after the hapless Frenchmen. Coming out of the snow, the Russian cavalry pounced upon Augereau's men long before they could react and form square. Behind them came two columns of green-coated Russian infantry.

As the first fugitives came flying back to the main line, Napoleon realized that this was a crisis of the first magnitude. He

The Eylau campaign

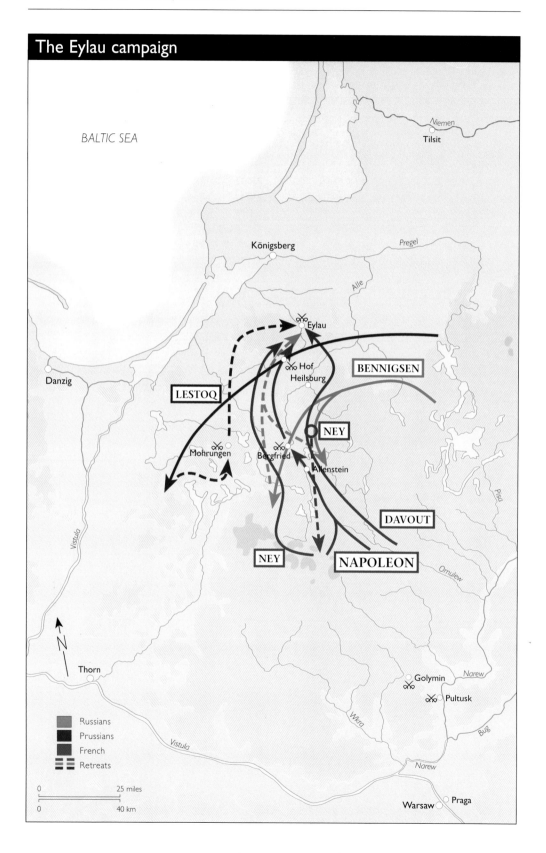

BALTIC SEA

Tilsit

Niemen

Königsberg

Pregel

Alle

Eylau

Hof
Heilsburg

BENNIGSEN

LESTOQ

Danzig

NEY

Mohrungen

Bergfried

Allenstein

DAVOUT

Vistula

NEY

NAPOLEON

Omulew

Pisa

Thorn

Golymin

Narew

Pultusk

Russians
Prussians
French
Retreats

Wkra

Bug

Vistula

Narew

0   25 miles

0   40 km

Warsaw   Praga

ordered Murat to send in his cavalry to right the situation. As the courier rode off, Russian infantry pushed into Eylau itself. The Emperor was within a moment of capture when his duty squadron charged these foes. The French were outnumbered beyond all hope, but they were able to blunt the attack until the Imperial Guard infantry arrived to hurl the Russians back.

What followed was the greatest cavalry charge in history. Murat's 10,700 men, making up 80 squadrons of line and guard cavalry, were sent forward in successive waves. The first hit the Russian infantry and cut into the army center. Here they overran several batteries before being stopped by the second line. The survivors of the first Russian line had lain down to let the French horsemen pass over them. Once clear they had stood, turned and fired into the cavalry's back. It was this type of behavior that had so often caused the French to forgo taking prisoners. This time the French took full revenge, for no sooner had the Russians stood and begun to fire than the second wave of Murat's cavalry hit. This time it was the Guard. It struck the enemy in the rear and cut a bloody swathe through the line.

The Russians now committed a further cavalry reserve to stabilize the situation. These men got the worst of it as the final wave of the French charge hit home. But following the rout of the Russian cavalry, and finding himself increasingly surrounded by squares of enemy infantry, Murat retired; his job was done, the crisis of the battle had passed.

Murat's epic charge allowed the less impetuous Davout's attack to develop and the initiative swung over to the French. By

The Battle of Eylau (by Gros). After the battle, Napoleon surveys the field. Such cold and slaughter the French army had not experienced before. (AKG London)

1 pm, Davout had launched his attack with the support of St Hilaire's division from Soult's 4th Corps. The attack progressed as planned and the left flank of the Russian army was bending back. The heroes of Auerstädt looked like winning another improbable victory. Napoleon was following the action, but was worried that Ney had not yet made his appearance. Further, the Prussians under Lestoq, who were being pursued by Ney, were unaccounted for. As night fell, Napoleon's worst fears were realized. Lestoq arrived on the battlefield and at just the right place. Seemingly out of nowhere, his men fell upon Davout's exposed flank. The tired veterans fell back to the protection of several villages. Had the Prussian attack not come, Davout would have maintained his position astride the Russian line of retreat. The Russian army had been saved by the last remnants of the once proud Prussian army.

Ney had been trailing Lestoq for several days, but had pursued a rearguard that had been meant to draw him away from the field of Eylau. The orders sent to him by Napoleon had been lost. As he marched down the road, a corporal called to the Marshal's attention the battle going on in the far distance. Deciding to march in the direction of battle, he finally arrived at 7 pm. Ney attacked with his lead element. He took the town of Schloditten, but soon gave it up, not knowing the position of all the troops around him in the winter night.

Eylau had been a bloodbath of the highest magnitude. Napoleon suffered over 25,000 casualties, the Russians about the same. The following day, out of ammunition and supplies, Bennigsen retreated on to his supply line. Napoleon gladly let him go. The Emperor was shaken by the carnage that his army had experienced and knew that he would have to refit before once more taking on the Russians. He retired into his winter quarters and called up more reserves to the front.

Both sides tried to put a positive spin on the outcome of Eylau. Austria wavered and considered once more entering the war. Only the 'Peace Party' headed by the Archduke

Charles prevented this action. Francis decided upon waiting to see the outcome of the next great battle. Napoleon offered Prussia a separate peace, which would restore all of Prussia east of the Elbe river. The King was initially disposed toward this, but his Foreign Minister, Hardenberg, opposed the offer and won over the King. War to the death seemed the only option. Europe waited anxiously for the resumption of the campaign.

Both armies spent the winter months refitting and resting. Two operations took place during the spring of 1807. Marshal Mortier had hemmed in the Swedes in Swedish Pomerania. When he marched towards Colberg with half his command, the Swedes attacked and drove back the remaining troops. Mortier rallied and in a series of running battles drove the Swedes back into Stralsund. The King of Sweden, who had lost his British support, had enough and signed an armistice on 29 April.

In March, Marshal Lefebvre invested Danzig. In perhaps the hardest-fought siege outside Spain, the city finally surrendered on 27 April. Now only Colberg held out. This could be invested much more economically than the other two cities and many of the siege troops were second rate.

The tidying up of the rear area let Napoleon plan his next offensive. Six days before he was to launch it, Sweden repudiated the armistice and renewed hostilities around Stralsund on 4 June. Next, on the 5th, Bennigsen struck, initially attacking Bernadotte and wounding him in the process, then he turned his main attention to Ney's corps. Alerted to what was coming, Ney, the master of the rearguard, drew the Russians slowly forward. While this action was happening, Napoleon issued orders to Davout to strike the Russians from the south. As the Russians took losses moving against the elusive Ney, Davout's attack got under way. Giving up, Bennigsen fell back and left Bagration as a rearguard. The wily Prince once more got the most out of his men and over a two-day retreat allowed the main army to fall back to their prepared position at Heilsberg.

Heilsberg

On 10 June, the lead elements of Napoleon's army, under Murat, arrived and attacked the outlying villages south of Heilsberg. The first village was taken, but the town of Bevernick proved more difficult. Soult's corps was committed to the fight. Forming a battery of 36 guns, they pounded the Russian avant-garde and Bagration's men were forced back. The Russians fell back contesting every foot of ground, but finally gave way and fell behind the main position. Here stood two Russian divisions in entrenchments backed by cavalry.

The French reorganized and made an assault against the Russian left. The key redoubt was taken at bayonet point. However, before more support could come up, the Russians counter-attacked with six battalions and threw out the enemy. Simultaneously, Prussian cavalry moved to the Russian infantry's right and, charging through the smoke, caught Espagne's cuirassiers at a standstill. The impetus behind them, the Prussians exacted their revenge for Jena. Many of the French were killed before they could ride off.

Another attempt was made to retake the redoubt, but once more the effort failed. All along the line, the Russian artillery blasted the French from the safety of their dug-in positions. At last the French fell back safely out of cannon shot.

At dusk, Lannes made one more effort to unhinge the Russian position. One of his divisions under General Verdier moved from

Heilsberg. The 55th Line have one of their Eagles captured by the Prussian 5th Hussars (by Knotel). (Author's collection)

the cover of the woods, came on at the double and fell upon the men defending the Russian line. Engaged in a vicious hand-to-hand fight, Verdier's men too were defeated when no support came to back up their initial success.

Heilsberg had been a needless bloodbath with the French taking over 8,000 in losses and the Russians probably something slightly less – needless because the following day the Russians were turned out of their trenches by a flanking maneuver. This battle might have had significant political effects had it not been for the events in the following few days.

At midday on 11 June, Bennigsen abandoned his position and fell away to the east. Convinced that his opponent would try to defend Königsberg, the last city of Prussia, Napoleon began to march his army in that direction. Throwing Lannes and the cavalry under Grouchy out towards Friedland, he got reports on the 13th that there was a large Russian presence in that area. Ordering the corps of Mortier, Ney, and the Guard to move to Lannes's support, he hoped that Marshal Lannes could hold on until the main army arrived.

Friedland

On 14 June, the anniversary of Napoleon's victory at Marengo, the battle started early in the morning. Bennigsen had crossed most of his army to the west of the Alle river. He thought he had caught one of Napoleon's corps isolated and viewed this as the opportunity to gain the victory that would bring Austria back into the war. At 2 am, the fighting began on both flanks. Bagration tried to push part of Oudinot's grenadiers out of the Sortlack forest. These elite troops were more than a match for Bagration's hard-fighting veterans.

On the northern flank, General Uvarov and the Russian Guard cavalry were attacking Grouchy's cuirassiers and dragoons divisions, with the support of more light cavalry. This was one of the great cavalry

fights in history, with the gallant French throwing back twice their number throughout the morning. Sending forward infantry support, the Russians seized the key village of Heinrichdorf. Grouchy countered by sending Nansouty's cuirassiers forward in a perfectly timed charge that caught the Russian infantry by complete surprise. The French quickly riding among them, most were sabered where they stood. Lannes now sent his reserve brigade of grenadiers to occupy the bloody streets of Heinrichdorf.

By 7 am Mortier's men began to arrive. Sent to the hardest-pressed part of the line, they frustrated every success that the Russians gained. The forest of Sortlack would change hands at least five times, but by 11 am it was firmly in French control. Nine hours had passed and Lannes had held out against almost three times his number. Bennigsen now made one more supreme effort to break the French, only to be hurled back more viciously than before. The butcher's bill was rising for Bennigsen and he called off the attack. There are some reports that Bennigsen now experienced a gall bladder attack that incapacitated him. Report after report was sent to Russian headquarters that the French were pouring on to the battlefield, but no response came forth.

Napoleon arrived on the field at 12 noon and met with Lannes. The Marshal reported that the Russian position was divided by the swollen stream called the Mühlen Floss. Further, their only line of retreat over the Alle was by three rickety bridges. Napoleon couldn't believe his fortune. Carefully watching every movement of the enemy, he placed the troops of Ney's 6th Corps, Victor's 1st Corps, and the Guard into their positions to deliver the crushing blow. Shortly before 5 pm, Napoleon gave his signal to attack. Ney's men stormed out of the Sortlack forest and slammed into Bagration's men. The blow hit like a hammer and drove them back on to the town of Friedland. Trying to stabilize the position, Bagration threw his cavalry on to Marchand's division, but General Latour-

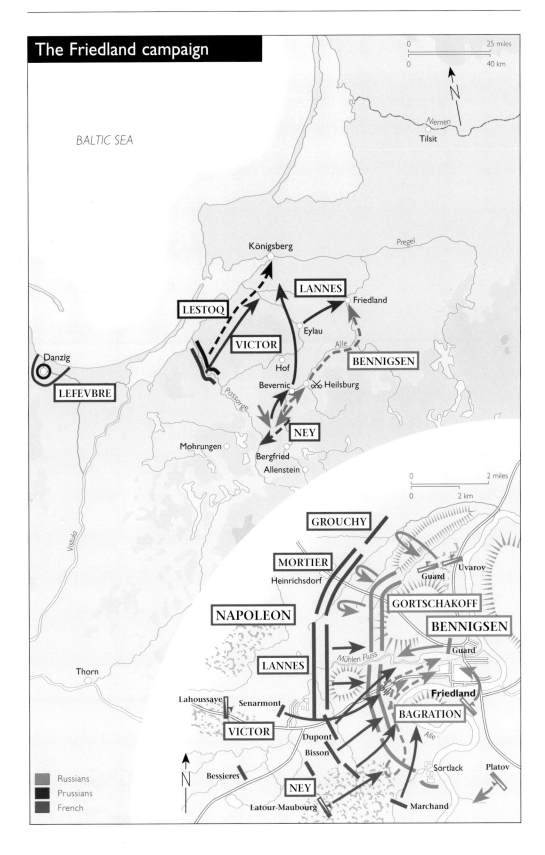

The Friedland campaign

BALTIC SEA

Niemen
Tilsit

Königsberg

Pregel

LANNES

Friedland

LESTOQ

Eylau

VICTOR

Alle

Danzig

Hof

BENNIGSEN

Bevernic   Heilsburg

LEFEVBRE

Passarge

Mohrungen

NEY

Bergfried
Allenstein

Vistula

GROUCHY

MORTIER

Heinrichsdorf

Guard   Uvarov

NAPOLEON

GORTSCHAKOFF

BENNIGSEN

Thorn

LANNES

Mühlen Fluss

Guard

Lahoussaye   Senarmont

Friedland

VICTOR

Dupont

BAGRATION

Bisson

Alle

Bessieres

Sortlack   Platov

NEY

Latour-Maubourg   Marchand

Russians
Prussians
French

Charge of the 4th Hussars at Friedland. The Hussars thought their swaggering panache made them the elite of the cavalry in every army. Their critics retorted that this characteristic was evident off the battlefield more often than on it. (Roger-Viollet)

Maubourg was waiting for such a move and rode down the Russians from the flank.

Ney's men pressed on, but were soon caught in a crossfire coming from the guns in front of Friedland and from across the river. Staggered by these blows, they then had to face the Russian reserve cavalry. Most regiments broke and ran. The Russian cavalry retired behind the rapidly contracting Russian center. Ney rode back and forth rallying his men and forming them back up for a final push.

As this was going on, Dupont, leading the 1st Division of Victor's corps, advanced and poured a galling fire into the massed Russians. Supporting him was Victor's chief of artillery, General Senarmont, with 30 guns. Rolling up to within close canister range of the massed Russian infantry formations, they unleashed salvo after salvo upon the hapless troops. In the smoke and confusion, the troops being so efficiently butchered could not even locate the source of their torment. Thousands died in place.

Napoleon now massed his howitzer batteries to drop shells on the town and bridges of Friedland. Soon all were on fire and in various stages of destruction. Bennigsen threw in his last reserve in the sector of this field, the Imperial Guard. Senarmont swung his guns about and swept away the cavalry in short order. The Guard infantry came on though and were met with sheets of flame as Dupont's men delivered a short-range volley. The giants of the Tsar fired back, but Dupont's men had seen much worse than this and, after wearing them down with an exchange of fire, leveled their bayonets and charged. The sight of these men coming on, having no respect or fear for their status, unnerved the Guard, who broke and fled into the overcrowded streets.

Ney's men were now pressing the advance and caught the Tsar's men against the Alle

Napoleon on the battlefield of Friedland
(by Vernet). Unlike Eylau, this was the decisive
victory Napoleon had come to expect. (AKG London)

river. Many jumped into the river trying to
escape the Frenchmen's fury. Terror seized
Bennigsen's men, and many who did not
surrender were slaughtered or drowned.

To the north, Lannes and Mortier now
advanced against the remaining Russians.
With their backs to the river, the men in
General Gortschakoff's column held on with
a fanatical desperation. If it had not been for
an opportunely discovered ford and the
inactivity of Grouchy's exhausted cavalry,
the result would have been the same as at
Friedland. As it was, fewer then half of
Gortschakoff's men could muster the
following day.

Friedland had been as complete a victory
as Napoleon would ever have. While taking
about 10,000 in losses himself, he had
inflicted nearly 40,000 on the Russians.
Alexander's army under Bennigsen was in
ruins. Five days later, Alexander requested an
armistice in preparation for a final peace.

The Treaty of Tilsit, 1807

On 25 June at Tilsit, the Tsar met with
Napoleon to make peace and divide up
Europe. Prussia was left out of the initial
negotiations.

The meeting was held on a raft in the
middle of the Niemen river. Napoleon had a
profound effect on Alexander personally. He
was generous to his vanquished foe and the
treaty granted Alexander much more than he
could have hoped for after such a crushing
defeat as Friedland. The provisions of the
peace were: the recognition of all the
territorial acquisitions of France and her
allies; the restoration of at least a truncated
Poland in the form of the Duchy of Warsaw
under the protectorship of the King of
Saxony; an alliance between France and
Russia; and the cession of the former
Prussian territory of Bialystock to Russia.
Napoleon abandoned the Turks and

recognized Russia's right to take the Danubian provinces away from his former ally. The peace treaty with Russia was signed on 9 July and that with Prussia on 12 July.

Much has been written about Napoleon's callous behavior towards the Turks, but this criticism fails to take into account the fact that the Sultan Selim III had been murdered the month before by his Janissary guards, who supplanted him with a puppet ruler, Mustapha. Selim had been a friend to Napoleon, and there was no reason for Napoleon to have any faith in Mustapha, for Selim was killed in large part because of the modernizing reforms he had introduced with the urging of French advisers.

Tilsit. On a raft in the Niemen, the two Emperors, ostensibly now allied, discuss the government of the world. (Hulton Getty)

Napoleon reviews the Russian Guard at Tilsit (by Debret). The new alliance even led to giving decorations to former foes, but the new friendships were not to last. (AKG London)

Prussia was humiliated. She lost all her holdings west of the Elbe and her Polish provinces. Furthermore, Danzig was declared a free city, to be garrisoned by the French. The beautiful Queen Louisa tried to use her charms upon Napoleon in order to ameliorate the conditions, but failed.

Sweden had been promised British support. What came was much too small to face the troops freed up from the victory at Friedland. With designs elsewhere, the British pulled out leaving the hapless King to face the might of France. The Tsar abandoned Sweden and Napoleon gave him permission to take Finland from her. This offer Alexander gladly accepted.

Lannes, Marshal of France

Jean Lannes was insecure, crude, blunt and reckless, but he may have been Napoleon's greatest marshal.

Early life and career

He was born in Lectoure, France, on 10 April 1769, four months before Napoleon. His family were farmers and Lannes received his basic education from his older brother, a priest. Apprenticed as a dyer, he gladly joined the local volunteer regiment in 1792.

His early combat experience was on the Pyrenees front, fighting the Spanish. Here he rose rapidly in rank, reaching that of colonel just over a year later. This early part of his career was highlighted by continual acts of bravery. In 1795, as the war with Spain was winding down, Lannes was placed under the command of General Pierre Augereau, the future marshal. Once more his outstanding combat performance brought him to the attention of his commanding officer. This began a friendship that would last for the rest of Lannes's life.

The division was transferred to Italy, and Lannes came under the command of Bonaparte when the latter took command of the army in March 1796. Napoleon first noticed Lannes when he led the decisive bayonet charge to win the Battle of Dego. Promoted to the command of the elite grenadiers, Lannes once again carried the day with his courage at Lodi, when he led the rush over the bridge that conveyed Bonaparte one step nearer to immortality.

When he performed almost the identical act at Bassano, becoming wounded in the process, Bonaparte promoted him to general. Recuperating, Lannes hurried to the front upon hearing news of the defeat at Caldiero. Finding that Bonaparte had regrouped to

conduct a flanking battle at Arcola, Lannes resumed his command. Being wounded twice more, he rose from his ambulance bed upon hearing of the continued failures of the army. He arrived at the front just as Bonaparte had been personally thrown down a steep bank into the river, amidst the confusion caused by a failed attack over the bridge of Arcola. Rallying the men, Lannes led the charge that took the town, and saved Napoleon from capture or death. This act earned him the eternal affection of the future Emperor.

The remainder of the war in Italy saw Lannes perform diplomatic missions to the Papal States and Genoa. In both cases, Lannes shocked the opposing diplomats by his bluntness, but came away with the desired outcome.

When Bonaparte led the campaign to Egypt, Lannes followed. After the victory of Alexandria came the march to Cairo. Murat complained bitterly about the conditions and Bonaparte's mistakes. When these grumblings got back to Napoleon, Murat blamed Lannes. This started a life-long feud between the two men.

Lannes continued to cover himself with glory throughout the Egyptian campaign. His one failure was at Acre, where he led an assault on the walls. Shot through the neck, he almost perished. Fortunately, he was dragged to safety by one of his officers. He slowly recovered, and did not see action again until he captured the Turkish camp during the victory at Aboukir. It was following this triumph that he learned that his wife had given birth to an illegitimate child. This made the moody Gascon even more so.

He had become one of Napoleon's closest friends, so it was not surprising that he was one of the few chosen to accompany

Bonaparte back to France. He played a small but important role in the coup d'état of Brumaire that put Napoleon in control of the government of France. Following this event, Lannes divorced his wife and prepared to rejoin the army.

In the campaign of 1800, Napoleon turned his attention to ending the war and retaking Italy. Lannes received the key command of the avant-garde. After crossing the St Bernard Pass through the Alps, Lannes's men swept down the Aosta valley. After several successful skirmishes, Lannes daringly led his men past the impregnable Fort Bard in the middle of the night. At Chiusella, Lannes led a storming party that seized the vital stronghold. This opened the line of communications and his men were resupplied. Under his leadership, his men continued to march quickly and took the city of Pavia. Moving south, he defeated the Austrians at Stradella.

He had now marched around the Austrian army and so turned back to the west to link up once more with the main army. As he approached the town of Casteggio, he saw on the heights above twice his number of enemy. Confident of his men, Lannes launched an

attack up the slopes. In a desperate struggle, the Austrians were pushed back, but had their numbers doubled by reinforcements hurrying up from the town of Montebello. The situation was critical, with Lannes riding up and down the line encouraging his men to hold on. On the verge of collapse, Lannes was relieved by the division of Victor, which was double-timing it down the road. They threw the white-uniformed Austrian infantry back to the town of Montebello.

After a lull of an hour, Lannes sent his men forward once more to double-envelop the village. Despite the commanding strength of the Montebello position, the French were irrepressible. The ground fell away sharply, and the retreating Austrians were caught with no good retreat route. Against odds of one to two, Lannes had won his signature battle. In 1808, he would be made the Duke of Montebello.

He enjoyed little respite, for five days later he and his men were fighting for their lives on the plains of Marengo. Here his troops resisted stubbornly for most of a day, but ultimately gave way. Finally, with new troops arriving on the field, Napoleon gave the orders for the counterattack that would win the day and regain Italy.

Following the Italian campaign, Napoleon rewarded Lannes with command of his Guard. He landed himself in hot water almost immediately by spending 300,000 francs out of the Guards' treasury to upgrade the men's condition. This came to the attention of General Bessières, who told his close friend Murat. The latter, itching to get back at Lannes, told First Consul Bonaparte. Infuriated, Bonaparte demanded that his friend repay the funds out of his own money or face court-martial. It was his old friend Augereau who loaned Lannes the money to get out of his fix. Lannes resigned his command of the Guard, but soon received the important diplomatic mission

Jean Lannes. Combining a shrewd tactical skill with astounding personal bravery, he was forgiven exceptional familiarities with Napoleon because of his battlefield prowess. (Ann Ronan Picture Library)

to Portugal. Remarried, Lannes headed south from Paris.

It was in Portugal that Lannes was able to win many trade concessions for France and, either from bribes or gifts, raised enough money to repay Augereau. Because of the success of his entire career, Jean Lannes was made one of the original 18 marshals in 1804. Recalled to Paris, he attended Napoleon's coronation before taking command of the newly formed 5th Corps at the camp of Boulogne.

Lannes in the Napoleonic Wars

This takes us up to the point where Lannes begins to appear in the earlier chapters on the campaigns of 1805-07. Lannes's V Corps was usually in the forefront of the *Grande Armée*.

Though Lannes was a very forthright personality, very prone to lose his temper when he felt put upon, he was capable of rising above it when necessary. Despite his

animosity for Murat, Lannes gave him his best support when Murat's cavalry trapped the Austrian column at Wertingen. When Murat followed the wrong trail before Vienna and had to recuperate by stealing a bridge across the Danube, Lannes was at his side to overawe and bamboozle the Austrian bridge guards. By the time the guards realized that they had been taken, French grenadiers were within the defenses. Seldom have such high-ranking officers been ready to lead special operations from the front-line. Because Murat in turn fell for the ruse of a false armistice, Lannes was robbed of enough daylight to destroy Bagration's rearguard at Schongrabern.

Before Austerlitz Lannes fell out with Soult after the latter had put him up to challenging

Lannes at Ratisbon, 1809. When several assaults had failed to take the walls and his men would not go forward, Lannes seized a ladder himself. Shouting to his men, 'I was a grenadier before I was a marshal,' he headed towards the walls. He was overtaken by his men, who soon captured the town. (Ann Ronan Picture Library)

Napoleon's plan but then backed down when the reaction was very hostile. After a hard fight on the northern flank under the insufferable Murat, Lannes thought his achievements were underrated in the victory bulletin compared to those of the despised Soult. Lannes stormed off from the army, and no one dared tell him to return.

The "AWOL" marshal rejoined his corps on the Prussian frontier on 7 October 1806, the same day that war was declared. Three days later he crushed the corps of Prince Louis at Saalfeld, beginning the cascade of French victories. For only 172 casualties, 900 Prussians and Saxons were dead including their leader, 1800 more were captured, and 6000 scattered, even though they were good troops. Training and leadership made the difference.

Lannes was first up the escarpment at Jena, and on 13 October he was in the forefront of battle the entire day, until the French army had gained another great victory. Without sleep or rest, his corps went on to round up the scattered Prussian survivors. In fact Lannes kept pushing all the way into Poland, though as winter closed in, the mud and cold slowed V Corps. In the end it took an entire Russian army to stop him at Pultusk, though in a desperate battle he tried hard to break through that as well. Finally the pace was too much for him, and he was sent on sick leave to Warsaw for his wife to nurse him back to health. She did a good job, despite depression caused by what he saw as the intrigues of jealous rivals, for in the spring he was in his best form. He skillfully held the Russian army in play at Friedland until Napoleon could bring up enough troops to launch a decisive attack. When the moment came, Lannes led his corps from the front, and the day ended in another glorious victory.

For once Lannes was satisfied with his share of praise and rewards, and he enjoyed several months in France with his family. He was called to action once again when the best generals were needed in Spain to repair the damage caused by lesser ones. Lannes was not even given time to gather his baggage, but literally had to gallop the length of France to get to his new command. Within days he was leading it into combat at Tudela on 23 November 1808. Catching a Spanish army unready, deployed over far too great a distance, he took the opportunity to crush one half while the other looked on aghast. When Lannes's attention shifted their way they ran. Lannes moved on to Saragossa, where fanatical resistance and demoralized troops had led to a series of costly and botched attempts at siege. Despite difficult conditions, Lannes revitalized the attack in this hardest form of warfare, street fighting against a determined foe.

Victory came, but at a terrible cost for besieger and besieged. It was a hard job well done, but observers remarked that Lannes was now war weary and depressed. His spirits rose when news came of battles on the Danube front. Lannes leapt at this chance to rejoin his beloved commander, Napoleon, and once more galloped the length of Europe to get there in time. He was one of the few French commanders to leave Spain with his reputation enhanced.

In 1809 he fought the Austrians once more, crowning a legendary career with more victories and acts of heroism. Before the walls of Ratisbon (Regensburg), when the troops hung back, he grabbed a ladder and tried to scale the walls himself. Leading from the front was his one military vice. After a dogged defensive action around Essling in May, Lannes paid for this when he was mortally wounded.

Lannes had been one of the few men who could speak to Napoleon on intimate terms, and never thought his respect for Napoleon should prevent honest criticism. Napoleon could never replace him. He died with a record of no defeats on the battlefield, and more than enough victories. His battle record was enough to cover the Arc de Triomphe by itself. He had grown from being a brave uncouth grenadier to being a man highly regarded for both his personal and military virtues. So much had he grown that Napoleon said of him after that "He had found a pygmy and lost a giant."

Art in the Empire

The Empire embraced and appropriated a number of artistic influences that had begun before and during the French Revolution. Naturally, the arts often reflected Imperial tastes, which approved of the fascinating and exciting interplay of Neo-classicism and nascent Romanticism.

Painting and music

In the field of painting, artists such as Jacques-Louis David and Antoine-Jean Gros not only reflected the epic glory of the Empire, but also expressed some of its highest sentiments. Music saw the movement from the strict classical style of Franz Joseph Haydn to the more lyrical strains of Romanticism. Ludwig van Beethoven became both the embodiment and the catalyst of this transition. His career would reflect the changes in music better than any other composer. A fervent republican the whole of his life, he composed Symphony No. 3 (the 'Eroica') in Bonaparte's honor, but changed the dedication 'to the memory of a great man' when he heard of Napoleon becoming Emperor.

The court of Napoleon saw a number of composers of whom none but the most scholarly of musicologists would know today – Mehul, LeSueur, Cherubini and Gossec. Napoleon's preference was for Italian-style opera, so that was what was most presented in Paris. This operatic era marked an interregnum period between Mozart and Verdi with little to distinguish it. However, not surprisingly, Napoleon's composers did produce some great martial music. Departing from the preceding fife and drum style, the Napoleonic army bands came close to approaching a modern orchestra. On the day of battle, the sound of 100 drums with accompanying brass would soar over the battlefield and provide an important boost for the morale of the soldiers.

Sculpture and architecture

Other arts flourished as well. Napoleon had opened the Louvre to the public to see the art from the collections of the Bourbon kings and from the spoils of Napoleon's first Italian campaign. Here was the sculpture of antiquity that had graced the palaces of Italian princes and Popes, as well as new masterpieces by contemporary artists such as Antonio Canova. The new public museum was organized by Dominique-Vivant Denon, the father of the modern museum system. Expanding upon ideas being developed in Vienna, Denon perfected the system of organizing the museum into periods of art and styles. Prior to Denon, pictures and sculptures had been presented in a hodgepodge fashion.

The Consulate and Empire saw a building program such had never been seen before in France. Paris witnessed the start of the Arc de Triomphe, the Bourse, the arcades along the Rue de Rivoli, the north wing of the Louvre, the Place Vendôme with its triumphal column, and the reconstruction of the Madeleine church. When you look on modern Paris, much of what you see was the Emperor's inspiration. While the works program in Paris is the most celebrated, Napoleon executed similar programs elsewhere in France.

French society

The society of France was transformed under the Empire. During the Revolution, much of what was considered high society revolved around the private salons, but in the early Empire the places to be were the courts of the Empress Josephine or one of Napoleon's sisters. This allowed Napoleon better to influence the politics and fashions of Paris.

Fashion had become more conservative after the libertine days of the Directory, which Napoleon found in poor taste. Women wore long, high-waisted, 'empire-style' dresses that were meant to hark back to the classical period of Greece. The men wore variants of the topcoat, vest and trousers. These were essentially the beginning of modern styles of men's dress.

It became fashionable to dine out for the first time in history. Restaurants had begun to flourish. France's first great chefs, Brillat-Savarin and Carême, were making their mark. The latter was Talleyrand's chef at the insistence of the Emperor, to employ the culinary as well as the diplomatic arts to enhance French prestige.

Napoleon put his stamp on everything from the theater to furniture, from the law to the Catholic Church. 'The Age of Napoleon' was as much a conquest of style and imagination as it was a military epoch.

Philippe-René Girault

Early life and career

Philippe-René Girault was a veteran by the time the *Grande Armée* marched eastwards in 1805. He joined the army in 1791 as a soldier-musician, probably aged 15. He served at Valmy and in the campaigns along the Rhine, enduring privations, enjoying adventures. By the time of Hohenlinden he was part of the band of the prestigious 5th Hussars, but soon afterward new regulations eliminated the cavalry bands. Musicians enjoyed to a limited extent the freedom of individual contractors, moving from regiment to regiment according to how much the colonel and officers wanted to subsidize the regimental music. Forced out of his billet in the Hussars, Girault drifted into a regiment that became the 93rd Line.

The 93rd was not a prestigious unit, but in its peacetime station it wanted a good band to impress the locals. Garrisoning La Rochelle and the Île de Ré in south-west France, the 93rd provided drafts for service in San Domingo, an unpopular duty where many perished from sickness. Not that the Île de Ré was much better, for it was a sickly station where many went down with fevers. Girault almost died, but he was nursed through the crisis by a girl whom he wisely married.

The Napoleonic Wars

Girault, his wife Lucile, and the 93rd Line were sent into Italy at the beginning of 1805 to provide a reserve for Massena's army. The regiment was a raw one and was not called into action, but Napoleon needed replacements to fill the gaps in his army after Austerlitz and Jena. In November 1806, the regiment was ordered to cross the Tyrolean mountains into Germany. The snow was deep, and even though Girault's wife was game, she was so short the snow came up to her thighs. She had to share a carriage with an officer's wife. The couple squeezed into an overcrowded inn in the mountains, but found they could not afford the wine or beer to go with what they had gathered for their dinner. A general of brigade chanced by, who happily invited himself to share their meal in return for providing the wine. The Giraults were happy: they calculated they had spent a mere 12 sous, whereas the General must have spent 6 francs or more.

Then it was down into Bavaria, where they settled into winter quarters in Augsburg. As Girault reported to his colonel in the city, a messenger told him that his wife, following the regiment on a *cantinière's* wagon, had fallen into the Danube when the carriage horse had panicked and gone into the river. Rushing back, he was relieved to find his wife being carried through the city gates: a *voltigeur* (the voltigeur company was the company specially designated for skirmish work) from the passing rearguard had gallantly leapt in and pulled her out of the river.

A *cantinière*, sometimes called a *vivandière*, was a soldier's wife or mistress working as a licensed sutler. Sometimes these women were very popular, especially if they extended credit, or were brave enough to bring brandy up to the regiment under fire. Under cannonfire or musketry, some *cantinières* were wounded or killed: some did not charge for brandy dispensed in action, thinking it part of their duty under fire. However, the *cantinière* riding with Lucile was obviously not one of these, because she was not popular. Perhaps because she did not extend credit or pressed her debtors too hard, or her protector might have been a bully. Whatever it was, none of the soldiers dived in to save her, and it was left to a Bavarian to fish her out.

The troops were never so happy as when they were campaigning in Bavaria or Austria. It was rich countryside in which to forage, even when the rations were regular. One officer thought that, whenever his battalion left a bivouac, it left enough food to last for 15 days. The soldiers hoped that by the time they had 'eaten' the country out, the supply services would have caught up. In billets the civilians were soon taught that if they did not serve their guests the best, the soldiers would not only help themselves, but cause waste and damage that would make it ten times worse. Of course, these habits did not make friends among the population, and the pickings were not so good in the poorer countries to the east, East Prussia and Poland.

At the end of a march, the fires were lighted, the camp kettles were put to the boil and some sort of shelter was improvised, as the army did not carry tents. Tents would slow up an army's march, and Napoleon's army marched hard. The troops had confidence in their leadership and accepted that hard marching resulted in fewer casualties. The French veteran Massena was admired for his ability to conjure shelters out of branches, straw, leaves, anything. Meanwhile, the marauders returned with food or wood for their comrades.

Recruits, however, would often arrive at a campsite so tired that they would just collapse, and unless there was someone to look after them, they would wake up to find they had to begin the next day's march after a night without warmth or food or shelter. After a few days of this, the conscripts would fall out with sickness and exhaustion, often being left to their fate and never seen again. The cold and mud of Poland, worse than they had ever seen before, soon showed the limitations of such a rough-and-ready style of warfare. The troops grew demoralized and losses from attrition soared. After Eylau, however, Napoleon pulled his troops back into warm

quarters and began to rebuild his army.

To replace the losses and reinforce the *Grande Armée*, rear area troops were brought up. In their wake, even second-line formations, like the 93rd, were called forward. In the spring of 1807, the regiment marched up to Berlin, being shocked on the way at how grisly the field of Jena was even six months later. Still stationed in Berlin, the regiment had comfortable billets and the chance for some tourism: Girault visited the palace of Frederick the Great. Then they went on to winter in Stettin, again in good billets.

Usually on campaign the troops did not have such amenities, but the French soldiers were famed for their ability to make themselves comfortable if they had a little time to do so. Further to the east, the *Grande Armée* was building itself military towns of wood, straw, and canvas in the wilderness near Tilsit. More than comfortable, the streets of these towns were even elegant. One regiment, to outshine its neighbors, planted rows of fir trees along their streets, one outside every hut. Then they built a parade ground, neatly bordered with more trees. Other regiments tried to compete, but soon there were no more woods within striking range. Even the villages had been dismantled to provide wood for the huts, after their barns and flocks had disappeared to feed the troops.

For an agrarian economy, one French soldier noted, 'War, flood, hail and fire are less dangerous than the presence of an enemy army.' Later this same soldier, Captain Elzear Blaze, saw his regiment reviewed by Napoleon himself, accompanied by the Tsar and the King of Prussia. The King was very impressed by the camp. 'It would be impossible to build finer camps than yours,' he said, 'but admit that you've left some wretched villages.'

But there was work for even a despised regiment. The 93rd was called forward to join Marshal Brune in front of the fortress of Colberg, and Girault had to leave his wife behind with their newly born son. This Prussian fortress had been under siege for some time, but as it was also a port, the

French land blockade did not work. Half-hearted attacks had only served to give the garrison a sense of heroism at being one of the few Prussian forces to hold out after the debacle of 1806. Brune, however, did not intend to sit in inactivity and ordered an assault. The 93rd went forward through a wood in a vigorous attack, but stalled. It sat exposed to the fire from the Red Fort to its front and from an English frigate cruising

The Camp of Boulogne (by Bellanger). While there were many ceremonies as illustrated here, usually the camp was the scene of constant training until the troops surpassed the standards of their opponents. (Hulton Getty)

along the shoreline to its left. The musicians wisely took cover behind some sand dunes, where the surgeon was working on the wounded streaming back.

As was usual, the band was conscripted to carry back the wounded. If there were limbs to be amputated, the surgeon worked away; other cases were loaded on wagons to be evacuated. Girault had never seen an amputation before; now he saw far too many. Soon he was covered in blood from head to toe, 'like a butcher,' he said. With the standards of medical care of the time, doctors resorted to amputation as the only answer to a shattered limb: if the doctor was skillful, the wounded might survive

operation and infection. A cannonball to head or body could only be lethal, a bullet wound might be survived if not in the gut or too deep, a saber wound was almost lucky.

When the regiment finally withdrew, Girault was left to watch some conscripted peasants dig a ditch to bury the limbs left behind. Seeing an arm on a pile of straw, Girault attempted to gather it up, but found it was still attached to its live owner. After his arm had been shattered, the poor soldier had made it as far as the surgeon, but had collapsed on a pile of straw. More straw and more wounded had been piled on top of him, and unconscious he had stayed forgotten until Girault found him. The

surgeon was summoned and amputated the arm. Not a single cry escaped the soldier, who ended up staggering off on his own legs to the hospital rather than await the return of an ambulance. Girault was impressed by this display of hardness, but in the days of the survival of the fittest, these soldiers were very tough – they had to be.

The next day the 93rd was allowed to stay in cover. An Italian regiment took its place in the line. A ration of beef was issued, but it was highly unlikely that the beef was in any recognizable cut, not unless a soldier had great pull with the butcher. When the regulations specified a pound of beef, they meant it literally, even if the pound included skin, bone or offal. Usually the beef was issued in one ration for a mess of soldiers, and often there was little they could do with it other than make it into soup or stew, not only because of the quality of the meat, but also because they seldom had more than a pot to cook in over an open fire. Occasional issues of rice or vegetables would make the meal more palatable, but usually a mess would have to scrounge or buy these. Sometimes the bread ration was so poor as to be good for nothing but a stew as well.

Girault and his fellow bandsmen had the makings for soup, but lacked wood for a fire. They went searching for it in the wood where the regiment had fought the day before. The garrison was still alert, and cannonballs soon chased the band to the cover of the sand dunes. Even there ricochets from the fire hunted them down, and they had to bolt for it. One of his comrades lost a thumb and finger, but Girault lamented more the loss of wood and soup.

After a hungry night, the next day the Peace of Tilsit was announced to the troops. The good news was tainted by a rumor that Brune had known of the peace three days earlier. In his quest for glory, Brune had proceeded with the attack anyway. Within a year Brune had been dismissed by Napoleon, probably for political reasons rather than this butchery. It had cost 400 unnecessary casualties, but the 93rd was finally blooded. That was the life of a soldier.

Conclusion and consequences

In the end, the Peace of Tilsit, negotiated in June and July 1807 between France, Russia and Prussia, failed to hold. Why was this? In essence, the stakes were too high for a compromise to endure. The conflict was always, ideologically, a war to the death. The old monarchies of Europe could not bring themselves to accept the principles of the French Revolution that Napoleon so represented to them, nor could they live with his domination of Europe. There were at least three successful imperialist powers, France, Britain, and Russia, each vying for the best position. This created an environment where the powers always looked for an opening to gain the advantage once more. The less successful imperialist powers of Prussia and Austria wished to revive their fortunes, and hoped to gain revenge for the humiliations they had received in 1805 and 1806 from this 'parvenu emperor'. They were potentially available as allies to Napoleon's enemies.

Napoleon would strengthen their resentment by instituting his Continental System. While it came close to driving Britain into bankruptcy, it also impoverished the mercantile economies that were under Napoleon's control. This led to widespread smuggling and defections. For example, as soon as the Treaty of Tilsit was signed, the Russian merchants aligned themselves with the established nobility to begin to undermine it. At sea, Britain enjoyed a domination that not only protected her, but gave her direct links to every continental power, and allowed her to strike at any coastline of Napoleon's Empire where an ally supplied an opening.

With an enormous empire to control, Napoleon had to incorporate more men into his army from outside France. Some new contingents did not have the enthusiasm for Napoleon that had driven his early armies. Furthermore, even the French recruits who took up the musket to replace their fallen comrades were now mostly conscripts. The French army no longer fielding volunteers, the rate of desertion increased. Finally, Napoleon's later armies never achieved the level of training that would have allowed them to perform the most intricate of maneuvers.

In the end, though, it may have been that the allies caught up with the French techniques for waging war on land. Captain Parquin, in his famous memoirs, tells of having a conversation with a Russian general following a French victory. 'The Russians are today pupils of the French, but they will end up by being the equals of their masters.'

Further reading

Bowden, Scott, *The Glory Years: Napoleon and Austerlitz*, Emperor's Press, 1997.

Chandler, David, *The Campaigns of Napoleon*, Cassell, London, 1997.

Duffy, Christopher, *Austerlitz 1805*, Cassell, London, 1999.

Elting, John R., *Swords around a Throne*, da Capo Press, USA, 1997

Esposito, Vincent J., and Elting, John R., *A Military History and Atlas of the Napoleonic Wars*, Greenhill Books, 1999

Hourtoulle, F.-G., *Jena, Auerstadt, the Triumph of the Eagle*

Petre, F. Loraine, *Napoleon's Conquest of Prussia 1806*, Greenhill Books, 1993

Petre, F. Loraine, *Napoleon's Campaign in Poland 1806-1807*, Greenhill Books, forthcoming

Jones, Proctor Patterson, *Napoleon: An Intimate Account of the Years of Supremacy:1800-1814*, Random House, USA, 1992

Thiers, Louis, *A History of the Consulate and Empire under Napoleon*

Vachee, Colonel, *Napoleon at Work*

Index

Other titles in the Essential Histories series

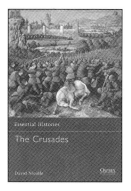

The Crusades

ISBN 1 84176 179 6
February 2001

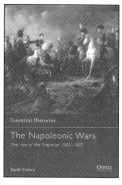

The Crimean War

ISBN 1 84176 186 9
February 2001

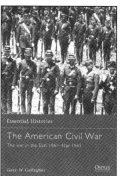

The American Civil War
The war in the East
1861–May 1863

ISBN 1 84176 239 3
February 2001

The Napoleonic Wars
The rise of the Emperor
1805–1807

ISBN 1 84176 205 9
February 2001

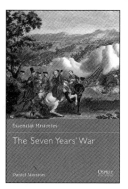

The Seven Years' War

ISBN 1 84176 191 5
July 2001

The American Civil War
The war in the East
1863–1865

ISBN 1 84176 241 5
July 2001

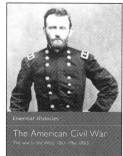

The American Civil War
The war in the West
1861–May 1863

ISBN 1 84176 240 7
September 2001

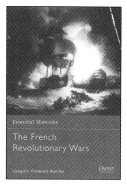

**The French
Revolutionary Wars**

ISBN 1 84176 283 0
September 2001

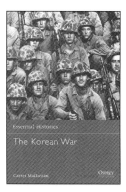

The Korean War

ISBN 1 84176 282 2
September 2001

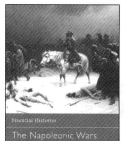

The Napoleonic Wars
The Empires fight back
1808–1812

ISBN 1 84176 298 9
September 2001

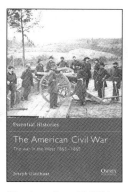

The American Civil War
The war in the West
1863–1865

ISBN 1 84176 242 3
November 2001

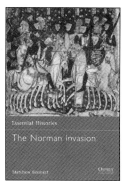

The Norman Invasion

ISBN 1 84176 228 8
November 2001